Volume two

Old Shoreham village & farms

before urbanization

Photographs and memories collected and presented by

Robert Hill
1996

ISBN 0 9525826 1 9

Page numbering continues from the first
volume which contains pages 1 to 68.

The photographs are individually numbered
and are located in the centre of the book.
Photos 1 to 64 are in the first volume.

Edited and published by Robert Hill, Copperfield, St. Nicolas Lane,
Shoreham-by-Sea, W. Sussex BN43 5NH

*Front cover: Gathering hay on Old Shoreham farm c.1916.
The name on the wagon is 'W.J. Norman Old Shoreham'.
Percy Norman was running the farm in 1916. See photo 70.*

*Rear cover: Old Shoreham bridge & Toll House, looking west c.1910.
Wreckage of Hawker Fury bi-plane on Mill Hill, 26 May 1932.
The pilot, Officer Jackson, was killed. See p.78.*

Books by post

Both volumes are currently available by post from R. Hill, to U.K. addresses only. Telephone 01273-461852 to check availability and cost, or enquire by post to address on previous page.

Corrections to first volume

Page 40. The Rawlings bought Lesser Foxholes before the war.

Page 45. Gumbrell should read Gumbrill.

Page 57. Wallace tractor should read Wallis tractor.

Photo 25. Mr. F. Witten advises that the young lady is not Hazel Frampton.

Additional information

Page 54. Mr. J. A. Hoare advises that the 1914-18 camp ground was not ploughed until the 1950's [ploughed land].

Photo 3. Mrs. D. E. Bishop says that James Duke is on the left.

Photo 22 was taken by Mr. B. A. Bazen.

Photo 25 was taken by Mr. F. Witten.

Photo 27 was taken by Mr. B. A. Bazen.

Photo 33. Mr. H. A. Baker says that the man on the engine is his father, Mr. R. J. Baker, and the man below on the right is Teddy Eames of 28 Ship Street. The owner of the engine is on the left.

Photo 41 is from the collection of Mr. H. A. J. Snelling.

Photo 52. Mr. J. T. Elliott advises that the tractor is an International Junior, imported from the U.S.A.

Photo 60. Mr. Len Tuppen says that the man is Harry Holmes.

Notes

(information given by interviewee)   [notes by R. Hill]

R. Hill would be pleased to receive additional information and see interesting photographs or documents. Telephone 01273-461852.

Mr. Leslie Pycroft (b.1927) lived on Connaught Avenue when the first houses were built there. He became an agricultural engineer.

Connaught Avenue. We moved to one of four new terraced houses when I was a year old. They were the first brick houses to be built on Connaught Avenue [which was then newly named and only went as far as the present Colvill Avenue]. Ours, named 'Connaught', now No. 92 Connaught Avenue, was close to and west of Slaters cottage [see photo 16], which was then unoccupied and derelict.

Slaters cottage was demolished soon afterwards, and two bungalows were built on the site. The floor sank a little in the front room of one of the bungalows because a well on the site of the old cottage had been filled with old rusty milk churns and similar debris, which eventually collapsed. [The well was in front of Slaters cottage.]

Elm trees. The lane from the old Post Office [see photos 11 & 12] continued past our house as a cart track to the gymnasium on the grammar school playing field [see photo 105] and Swiss Gardens. Outside our house, the lane consisted of small flints and black cinders. During wet weather, ducks used to swim on the large puddles which formed. Opposite our terrace, in the middle of the road, was a grassy bank with a row of large elm trees. They were very old. Some were little more than an inch thick in places where the tree was hollow. [Dwellings built opposite by 1931, were set back. You could walk either side of the trees.]

Elm trees felled. The elm trees were felled when the modern road was made in the [late] 1930's. My father took photos [see photo 74L] of the trees just before they were felled. The workmen were mostly Irish labourers. Whilst working there, some of the labourers slept in the thatched cottages on the corner [see photo 15], which were derelict then. The tree at the corner was taken down at the same time, when the corner was rounded off.

The dustman came with a horse and cart to collect our rubbish. The cart had shutters on either side, and a low rounded top. There was an access between our house and Slaters plot, with bushes and nettles at the far end, and an open field beyond. Within seconds of the dustman leaving the horse outside our terrace, it would make straight for the bushes for a quick feed, even though it had a heavy load to pull. This happened every week whilst the dustman went to each of the four houses to collect the bins. The air was frequently blue with shouts from the dustman, who had to carry our metal bin to where the horse had stopped and then return with it.

The meads. My mother took me along the cart track, or cinder path, to Miss Glazebrook. She ran a small private school on Victoria Road, in an upstairs room. I later attended Victoria Road school and remember playing with my friends in the meads. A lot of old trees grew around the perimeter banks. In winter the lower area was often wet and soggy.

Strong milkman. Batten's milkman in the late 1930's was a large, sturdy man. He had to be! He delivered the milk on a very heavy tubular framed tricycle with one wheel beneath the saddle and two in front. The front wheels supported a tubular steel basket which carried the milk bottles. This basket was about four feet square and 2 feet deep. The tyres were much wider than cycle tyres and it had a motor cycle chain. I tried to pedal that tricycle when I was 16 years old and I could hardly move it, even though empty.

Perryman's shop was just around the corner [see illus. 75]. I remember being allowed to buy sweets and lemon powder from there. All sorts of things were on sale. One could buy sweets for as little as a half penny, and quite a lot for two pence. There was a large orchard adjoining the shop, on the west side of Connaught Avenue. Mr. Perryman, the son, later ran a taxi; a Vauxhall 10.

Cycle repairs.   During the 1930's, Mr. Perkins repaired cycles and motor cycles in a corrugated shed which stood on the west side of Old Shoreham Road, opposite what is now the Amsterdam p.h. [see photo 68].

Scout meetings.   I often played around the hollow tree by the lych gate of St. Nicolas church. In the 1930's, I attended scout meetings at the old School House and went to camp at Wappingthorn Manor farm, Steyning.

Steyning Road. Charlie Miller occupied some land on the east side of Steyning Road. He cut bean poles and pea sticks and kept chickens and goats. He cycled there from his other property, which was on Old Shoreham Road. I believe he had poor eyesight because he wore thick glasses. Old Mr. Castle occupied land on the west side of Steyning Road, opposite Charlie Miller's, and cut timber into logs for the fires. They sold the logs from a horse and cart. There was very little traffic on the Steyning Road in those days and it was safe to walk along it.

The steam lorry from the cement works was a large vehicle with a rounded front, a funnel on top, and doors without windows. It came puffing along. Underneath the driver's cab, you could see the red hot cinders dropping into a large round tray. It had a chain drive, with links about 6 inches across. I believe the wheels were cast iron, with solid tyres. When I was a schoolboy, my mother took me to watch them blow up the old chimney at the cement works. That was on the west side of the Steyning Road. Lots of people watched.

Waterworks, brooks, chalk pit. The waterworks is now fenced in, but was open when we were children. To the north of the building there was a nice round pool where we got tadpoles. It was quite deep and the water was so clear that you could see the chalk [a spring]. Fresh water flowed out of there into the streams. There were lots of brooks in the flat area below Mill Hill. It flooded in the winter and never dried up in the summer. There is far less water in the brooks since the fly-over was built. The chalk pit is very overgrown now. During the war, two or three large concrete stores were built there, near the waterworks road. They had steel doors.

Very cold winters were common in those days and you could walk on the ice when the brooks froze. Thick ice sometimes hung from the branches of the trees. We got deep frosts which we do not see in the south now. Even the river Adur sometimes iced over near the banks. [The sea froze on parts of the Sussex coast in February 1929. It snowed every day from 18-25 December 1938. Along the coast, birds died of exposure and their bodies were washed up onto the beaches. The winter of 1939-40 was very cold for two months. A temperature of minus 21°C was recorded in December, then the lowest recorded for Sussex. On 27 January 1940 there was a spectacular glaze. Cold rain fell and encased everything in ice. Telephone wires snapped, and birds were frozen to the trees by their feet as they roosted. There was another bleak winter from January to March 1947. Information from The Sussex Weather Book.]

Wartime sand bags. At the beginning of the second war, in 1939, earth was dug from a long bank, on the west side of Steyning Road, to fill sand bags. It was quite a high bank. The bags were put up against buildings, such as Council buildings, to prevent damage from bomb blasts. They were also used by the army around sentry posts.

Old Shoreham farm

Collected milk & eggs. Living close to Old Shoreham farm, I used to collect our milk and eggs from Mrs. Frampton, who was always very kind to me, and I was often offered cake. I went in along a passageway on the north side of the farm house, between the cow shed and the house, and into a funny shaped room where they sold the milk and eggs.

The forge on St. Nicolas lane was one of my favourite places. I remember Mr. Tommy Mason, the farrier [see photos 19 & 36L]. I often stood and watched him at work. He was always very pleasant to me and would tell me what he was making, and how.

Collected cows. When I was about 13 years old I sometimes went with Mr. Boxall to bring in cows from the brooks along Steyning Road, and take them back again after their afternoon milking. This was either during the school holidays or at the weekend. To me, the cow shed was a warm and sweet smelling place, with the cows noisily chewing their hay, and their coats warm and soft. I believe they had about 30 cows and they were hand milked. Later they had more cows, about 50. The bull was housed on the left as you went into the upper yard [see photo 34], which is now converted to dwellings.

Sheep grazing. Mr. Frampton sometimes drove sheep past our house and through a gate at the end of Colvill Avenue, so they could graze on the grammar school playing field. I sometimes helped to remove fly strike maggots from the wool and skin of the sheep. The affected wool would come away and Stockholm tar was smeared over the area with a stick, to stop infection.

Ploughing & harvesting. I sometimes watched the ploughman driving the horses up and down the field north of Adur Lodge, where the horses now graze. At lunch time he rested under the hedge on the upper east side of the field, behind the houses, while the horses fed from nose bags. Occasionally I sat and talked with him during his break. The field was much larger before the A27 by-pass was built. Mr. Frampton grew root crops there, according to season, and frequently corn. After harvesting and stooking the sheaves, the villagers would glean spilt ears of corn from the ground for their own use. Later, the corn was loaded onto wagons and taken to the farm.

Picked clean. A hundred or more chickens would then be given free range on the field to pick up the remaining grains. A row of large four wheel chicken coops would be pulled into the field and placed along the southern edge, under the trees which run parallel with The Street. The hens were locked in the coops at night as a safeguard against foxes. A month or so later, they would be moved back to the farm.

A hay stack was usually built in the field opposite the reservoir, somewhere near the gate, at hay making time. I frequently wandered around on my own, and often stretched out on top of it.

Sheep minding. Occasionally, during the period 1939-43, I went up the hill to check the sheep with Mr. Frampton and his daughter, Hazel. We went in the old Austin 12/4. There was a worry that sheep might fall into army trenches which had been dug for training. Moss, the sheep dog, would nearly always attend. Sometimes, I was allowed to go to Beeding Court Farm with Mr. Frampton in the old Austin with a trailer of milk churns. The floor of the car usually had straw and earth on it. It often carried a lamb or calf inside. It was a plywood floor, and you lifted part of it to get to the battery. It was not cleaned very often, but the animal smell was not unpleasant to me. I enjoyed every moment and was a willing helper.

The downs

1914-18 army camp. The cutting through the downs for the A27 Shoreham by-pass went through the old army camp. The camp extended north about as far as the reservoir [but on the east side of the road]. There were no buildings left, just foundations and post holes. As children, we often searched there and found cartridge cases and brass buttons. [There was also a boxing ring cut into the chalk to the east of Mill Hill. That disappeared with the cutting for the by-pass]. During the 1914-18 war there were army camps behind Shoreham all the way from Mill Hill [east side of road] to Slonk Hill. After the 1939-45 war, the W.S.A.E.C. [West Sussex Agricultural Executive Committee] ordered the camp ground to be ploughed and cultivated.

Freedom on downs. During the 30's the downs were virtually unfenced, open land. North of the reservoir, and above the cement works, were thick clumps of blackberry bushes, with sizeable fruit. The local people gathered this freely during the season. I can remember being up there picking blackberries in wartime when there were aircraft overhead. During the second war the army had most of the land. The local people were allowed up there but anyone else needed a permit. The area on the east side of the road, up to the golf club, was restricted to army personnel.

Lambing. When Mr. Tuppen was the shepherd, I sometimes visited him at Mossy Bottom. He lived there during lambing time in a four wheeled shed or caravan, complete with a rough bed and a stove. He was always kind to me and explained what he was doing with the lambs. If I was lucky we would share a hot drink. The caravan had bales of straw around it, in the form of an enclosure, to help keep the cold wind off the sheep and lambs. He kept any delicate lambs with him, inside the hut. If a lamb lost its mother and another ewe lost its lamb, he would place the skin from the dead lamb onto the live one. The ewe would then recognise the smell and adopt the surviving lamb.

A shepherd's hut was sometimes put in the valley about midway between the reservoir and Mossy Bottom barn. We had some evacuees staying with us at the beginning of the war, and I took them there several times.

Agricultural engineer. During 1941 I became 14 years old and started work at Holloways Engineers, making aircraft and gun parts on a lathe and milling machine. That is now Frosts, on the Brighton Road. They had a garage, an agricultural department and a big machine shop. Later, I worked in the agricultural department, learning to repair machinery. I went with the mechanic to various farms. Holloways repaired steam traction engines for Findlaters; the wine merchants of Hove. Some of the men at Holloways were ex-navy men who knew all about steam. I enjoyed working with them.

Vintage car. Whilst clearing out an old building at Holloways, we found a 1904 'De Dion' car covered by years of dirt and junk. It was restored by Mr. 'Pickles' Knight, who was in charge of the vehicle department. I believe it is still being used on the London to Brighton annual rally.

Drove Frampton's car. I learned to drive on Mr. Frampton's Austin 12/4 when it was road tested after repair at Holloways. It was a very easy car to learn on. I remember driving it along Middle Road, which was very quiet then. At this time the old car was beginning to get very rough. The doors would not shut properly because of worn hinges, the tyres were very worn, and the prop shaft universals had little or no bearings left. Everything rattled, but the Austin was never difficult to start and in its time was a good work horse.

Tractor accident. Albert Longley, the carter, occasionally had to drive Mr. Frampton's tractor. Mr. Frampton replaced the old Fordson with a new tractor which had two foot brake pedals, one for each rear wheel. You pressed one or other pedal to make the tractor turn more sharply. I heard that Holloways had to recover the tractor one day from the ditch by the waterworks road. That may have been around 1943, because I was still at Holloways. Albert had turned to go through the gate into the field, used the foot brake, and ended up in the ditch because the new tractor had turned more sharply than he expected. The old tractors were started on petrol. When the engine was hot enough, it was switched over to T.V.O., tractor vapourising oil, a sort of paraffin.

Called up, then self-employed. I was called up to join H.M. Forces in 1945. On my de-mobilisation in 1948, I became a self-employed agricultural engineer and used an ex-army truck to visit nearby farms. In return for garage space at the farm, either in the lower yard [see photo 25], or in an open barn on the east side of the farm house, I gave Mr. and Mrs. Frampton's new Austin 16 a weekly check-over and greasing. They kept it in a lock-up on St. Nicolas Lane, behind the terraced houses, about opposite the steps into the farm house garden. [The steps can be seen in photo 17.]

Spare parts were a problem after the war. Many of the local farms still had only the old pre-war horse drawn reaper/binders; usually converted so they could be drawn by tractor. They were two wheeled machines made of wood, with horizontal bars which went round and swept the corn into the cutters. The machine then tied the corn into sheaths. I frequently had to go and repair old machinery because we could not get spare parts.

Hunter put down. Driving to Steyning one morning, around 1949, I recovered a shaking driver and damaged Standard 12 car on Steyning Road, just south of Old Erringham. Mr. Frampton's beautiful hunter had jumped out of the field into the path of the car. The hunter was found further along the Steyning Road and had to be put down. It was badly injured through putting it's hoof between the bumper and radiator grill of the car. I repaired the car.

Messerschmitt crash. During the war, I recovered part of an oxygen apparatus which had been shot from a Messerschmitt 110 by local fighter aircraft. The plane landed in the valley north of the old camp, between Mill Hill and Buckingham barn, but a little further north. I still have the part, which I found in the old camp. It was the bellows which fed oxygen to the pilot. I believe the fighters were Hurricanes stationed at Shoreham. The pilot of the Messerschmitt was O.K. but the other occupant was injured.

Bomber crash. A Hampden bomber crash-landed to the east of where the Mill Hill bridge now crosses the A27. The crew were not injured, and they all sat on the fuselage, above the cockpit, waiting to be collected by R.A.F. Truleigh. The bomber was facing west, presumably heading for Shoreham airfield.

A doodlebug, the German V1 flying bomb, passed the rear of our house in the latter part of the war, missed farmer Passmore's house at Coombes, and demolished an adjacent barn. He had a lucky escape.

A radio transmitter was housed in a round building in the middle of the field just beyond the car park to the north of the reservoir. At the request of R.A.F. pilots, their position would be transmitted to them. I sometimes visited the young air force operators and was allowed to listen to ground-to-pilot instructions. A small wheel turned the roof-top aerial for position finding.

I can look back on my childhood with great pleasure and happy memories of the village people of Old Shoreham and of the countryside.

My earliest memory is living with my mother and grandmother at 'Fair View', a three storey house on the east side of Old Shoreham Road, about 30 yards north of Freehold Street. My grandmother, Ada Funnell, rented the property from the Smart family, who owned the whole block. [The properties were just inside New Shoreham parish. Aston House flats are now built on the site.]

Mother visited weekly. My parents had split up, and my cousin Gerald Prince [b. 1920] was in a similar situation. He came to live with us at 'Fair View' in 1926 and we got on very well, like brothers. Our mothers had to get work where they could, generally in one of the big hotels in Brighton. On their days off, once a week, they would come to visit us at grandmother's. Our mothers could both play the piano, and we often sang songs.

Smith's fair. Opposite 'Fair View', between the road and the railway line, was a large open space; a wedge shaped garden. It was bought, in the mid 1920's, by the Smith family, who had a travelling fair. They hardened the surface by bringing in loads of chalk. The fair was stored there during the winter. The gate was opposite Freehold Street. At the north end of the site they built a log hut where they did the cooking. The Castle family, who went round with the fair, lived at the narrow south end of the site.

Cutting logs was one winter occupation for the men of the fair. The girls from the fair sold them for firewood from a horse and cart. My grandmother was a good customer, and I enjoyed seeing the girls at work.

The steam traction engines were overhauled by the men during the winter. We frequently went over there as children and saw the roundabout and other equipment being serviced. The roundabout was stripped, then re-assembled and re-painted. It had a steam organ in the middle. When the man came to tune the organ, the engine in the centre of the roundabout was steamed up. The tuner spent the whole day there and played a considerable number of tunes. Finally, when it was all working, we were given free rides.

Assembling the fair on the day before it left Shoreham, to start its summer round of fair grounds, involved a lot of interesting activity. The various trailers & caravans, and the centre of the roundabout, were pulled into place to make up the road trains for each steam traction engine to pull. The two biggest engines, 'Perseverance', which was mine in spirit, and 'Pride of the South', which was Gerald's in spirit, would be at the front, followed by a Tasker called 'Little Giant'. That was sometimes driven by Elizabeth, one of the younger fair girls, who was as able as the men at driving it. Very early the following morning, grandmother would waken us boys so that we could go to the front bedroom window and watch the fair leave.

Old Shoreham school.   I started at Old Shoreham school when I was just four years old [Jan. 1923], and I remember that Bob Bowyer, who was then aged about ten, took me there on my first day. We liked and respected our three teachers. Miss Archer, the head mistress, was nick-named 'Froggy' and took the senior class. Miss Young took the middle class. Miss Spragg, who took the youngest class, rode a motor cycle. That was most unusual for a lady teacher at that time.

Partitions between the classrooms were slid back during the nativity play, and during other events, so that the whole school could assemble. The piano had to be moved to a different position, usually by several senior boys. On one occasion it was lifted underneath the keyboard, which came away from the rest of the piano. Keys fell on the floor and the piano was useless. A small pedal pumped organ was borrowed from the church. This provided more entertainment as Miss Young had difficulty keeping up the air pressure.

Black faces.   When the school caretaker was laid up for a while, John Cooper and I were given the job of filling the classroom coal buckets, which we did after the afternoon break. We shovelled too hard and filled the air with dust. The other children were very amused when we came in with black faces.

The Royal Artillery was going along St. Nicolas Lane one morning when we came out of classes for our morning break. That was before Bypass Road was built, probably about 1926. The horses, riders & guns made a very interesting sight and some of us went for a closer look. One of the teachers brought us back.

Rev. Hughes came to help Rev. Glossop, the vicar, and took a lot of interest in us, as it was a Church of England school. One day he took a group of us boys to Worthing for a long day out. We assembled at school then marched to the railway station. We spent the morning on Worthing beach, throwing stones into the sea and generally having fun. It was a nice change from school.

Skating on the brooks.   One winter, when the brooks [Steyning Road] were frozen over, a large group of us went there to skate as soon as morning school finished. We called it skating but it was really running and sliding with our shoes on. We stayed there when we should have returned to school. Eventually one of the teachers came for us and we were all berated.

Aeroplane crash on Mill Hill.   Another lunch time escapade took place in 1932. We heard a lot of aircraft activity, followed by a thump. Later, we were told that an aeroplane had crashed on Mill Hill. We went rushing up there to look for souvenirs. The aeroplane was buried into the hillside, and the body of the pilot had been taken away. A policeman arrived and told us all to go back to school. We were talking about it for days afterwards. [On 26 May 1932, two Hawker Fury bi-planes collided in cloud. One crashed on Mill Hill and the pilot, Officer Jackson, was killed. See photo on rear cover. The other pilot parachuted to safety. A third Hawker landed on Mill Hill, east side.]

Choir boys wages. Gerald and I joined the choir at St. Nicolas church around 1928. We had to pass a test by singing solo to Mr. Glyde, the choir master. We were attracted by the pay of one shilling & sixpence [7½p] every three months, plus four pence every time we sang at a wedding or funeral. Another bonus was time away from classes on occasions.

Purple cassocks. In the early days, we wore a surplice and black cassock. We were pleased when this was changed to a purple cassock, white collar and purple bow tie. We felt very smart when we occasionally sang at St. Mary's church, because their choir boys still wore the black cassock. Later, Mr. Glyde was replaced by Miss Child; an elderly spinster who was very pleasant and sometimes held choir practices at her house in Buckingham Road, near the railway crossing. [Miss Child, 2 Buckingham Road, 1930 directory.]

Gas lamps. Choir practice was normally held at the church at 6 p.m. on Wednesday or Friday evenings. In the winter, Miss Child had to light several of the gas lamps so that we could read the music sheet. She had to turn the gas on at one side of a large pillar and go round the other side to apply the match. We occasionally turned the gas off before she could light it. If we were feeling very mischievous we did it several times in succession until she got very annoyed.

The organ had a long lever on the side, and a lead weight on the end of a length of string. If the weight dropped below a line marked on the organ, the music would fade. The handle had to be pumped up and down to operate the bellows and keep the weight above the line. For our amusement, and to the annoyance of the organist, we often waited until the music started to fade before pumping madly.

Several boys joined the army. My cousin Gerald [Prince] joined the Royal Navy around 1936 and was lost when the Royal Oak was sunk by a German submarine in 1939. A number of boys from Old Shoreham school joined the Territorial Army in 1936, including myself. We all joined together, and when the war came we were called up and served together for a time in the 57th Field Regiment, Royal Artillery. Ernie Cooper became the Sgt. Major. Some of the others were Alec Hancorn, John Minter, and Harry Baker.

Prisoner-of-war. Malcolm Langrish was in our unit but he got moved around and became a prisoner-of-war in Germany for 3½ years, after being captured in Crete. His mother was sent copies of the Red Cross journal 'The Prisoner of War' and she had them bound. Malcolm has recently sent them back from Canada.

Corrugated shed. Motor cycle repairs were done in the corrugated shed on the west side of Old Shoreham Road, opposite what is now the Amsterdam p.h. [see photo 68]. Richardson and Perkins did it as a hobby or sideline. They were both motor cycle enthusiasts. They kept their daytime jobs and opened it in the evenings and at weekends. Tom Perkins was a pattern maker at the Portslade gas works and became my father-in-law. He later ran the business with his brother at Ham Road, and they were joined by Mr. Robins. I worked there for a time. Behind what is now the Amsterdam p.h., there was a car scrap yard run by a Canadian named MacLeod.

Miss Jane Castle (b.1912) travelled around with Smith's fair as a child, and later lived on Steyning Road.

We went round with Smith's fair until 1931. After that we didn't do any more fairs. We were not with Smith's fair all the time; there were a couple of periods when we joined the London fair, but I was just a little girl then. From 1931 we lived on Steyning Road for 25 years, and I have been here at Smith's yard, Old Shoreham Road, for the last 30 years.

Smith's fair had a steam driven roundabout with an organ in the middle, swinging boats (not steam driven), shooters, touch-ems, hoop-la and all kinds. It was a typical fair; there was no show or circus with it. We travelled all over, not just Sussex, and the fair came back to Smith's yard for the winter. I ran the touch-ems, which consisted of 5 things on a plank. You threw 5 balls at them, and if you knocked down four you won a prize.

Tom Smith owned the fair and the roundabout. He also owned the steam traction engines which pulled the fair from place to place. We were what you called followers. Tom Smith was my uncle; he married my father's sister, Mary Ann Castle.

In the winter, we went round selling chopped logs for firewood. The men did any work they could get. There were only a few men. At the time I remember, most of the boys were at school in the winter. We all went together, to Victoria Road school. I only had one winter at Victoria Road school; I had another winter at Southampton, and another at Gosport.

Before we pulled in [i.e. finished with the fair] in 1931, we wintered in the yard to the north of the house on the west side of Steyning Road; the house nearer the fly-over. After we pulled in, we lived in the house; which was then known as No. 2 Steyning Road. It was changed to No. 3 when Valentine Close was built [c.1955].

My father was Henry Castle, and my mother Louisa. Her maiden name was also Castle because she married her cousin. I was born in 1912, and my younger brother Jimmy in 1919. From 1931, we lived at the house and Jimmy and I supported our parents until father could draw his pension, which was only ten shillings a week. When the war broke out, Jimmy went into the army and I went in the Land Army. My father died in 1959 and my mother died in 1961.

There were a number of Mary Castles because several of the brothers, 5 or 6 of them, had a Mary or a Jim Castle. The sisters Mary Castle [b.1920] and Freedom Castle [b.1918] who attended Old Shoreham school were the children of my uncle John Castle; my father's brother. He also travelled around with Smith's fair. They had an older brother Thomas [b.1917] and a younger brother Jimmy. We always called Mary 'Joker'. We all went separate ways after we finished with the fair. I would not know Mary now because she was very young when I last saw her [age 11 in 1931].

80

> Miss Lily Tubb (formerly Gadd) was born in 1923 at Old Erringham farm cottages. Her grandfather Stenning lived in the railway cottage on Old Shoreham Road.

Tubb alias Gadd. I was known as Lily Gadd when I was at Old Shoreham school, but we found out later that our name was really Tubb. My father, Percival Edward Tubb, had always believed his name was Gadd, but that was the name of his step-father. The mistake was discovered when my father needed a birth certificate for a job with Southern Railways. My younger sister Evelyn and I were christened as Gadd, and I was already registered at school as Lily Gadd, so we kept that name until we left school; meanwhile the official documents were altered.

Greenfield Cottage

My mother's parents, Stenning, lived at Greenfield Cottage, by the bend on the west side of Old Shoreham Road. They were there in 1910 when their youngest child, my aunt Rose, was born. She was a bit of a tearaway and went round with Smith's fair one summer. Greenfield Cottage was a typical single storey railway cottage with a veranda around it. The canopy of the veranda had a typical fascia of the type you see on railway stations, made of short vertical planks with a shaped lower end. It had cellars underneath which flooded when the tide was up. [The cottage is named Old Shoreham Cottage on the 1912 map, but was called Greenfield Cottage by 1914. From 1891-1901 it was occupied by Michael Bridle, a platelayer.]

The cottage had four rooms. So far as I remember, you could walk all round the outside, underneath the canopy. Going through the front door, there was a living room on the right [north] with a cooking range. At the back of that was another room which should have been the kitchen, but my grandmother had the range moved into the living room, probably for warmth. The old kitchen was used for preparing food and washing clothes. On the left [south] side were two bedrooms. There was no bathroom. The toilet was an earth closet in the garden, on the north side.

The ground level sloped down from the road towards the railway bank. There was a courtyard at the back of the cottage and you had to go down a number of wooden steps to get to it. Access to the cellars was from the courtyard. You had to go up some more steps from the courtyard to get to the garden, which curved right along by the railway line.

Railway ganger. Grandfather, James Stenning, worked as a 'ganger' on the Shoreham to Horsham railway line. He was a foreman in charge of a gang of men. When he retired, around 1935, they had to give up Greenfield Cottage to make way for the next man, Mr. Milham. The Milham's lived there for a long time. When they left it was in a poor state, mainly due to damp, and was demolished.

Mother worked at Ravenscroft. My mother, Lily Stenning [d.1986], the oldest child, had already left school when her parents moved to Greenfield Cottage. She worked at a large house called Ravenscroft, on Ravens Road, as a domestic servant for Mr. & Mrs. Dell. She was there for many years. I think she started as an under maid, later became parlour maid, and eventually the cook. She lived-in but went home frequently to visit her parents. She was there until she married my father.

Match maker. Grandmother Elizabeth Stenning [nee Sanford] was very friendly. She liked the garden and was often outside the cottage. I believe she got to know my father because he was working as a cowman at Old Erringham farm, and frequently drove the pony and trap along Old Shoreham Road with the milk churns. I believe that was father's first job after he left the army, probably in 1919. Grandmother liked my father and introduced him to mother. I believe they married in 1921. Great grandfather George Sanford was a shepherd. [He and his family were living at No. 10 The Street in 1891.]

Born at Old Erringham. My birth certificate shows that I was born at Old Erringham farm cottages in November 1923 [see photo 84]. My sister was born there two years later, in 1925. I was told we lived next door to the Wellsteads. I believe old Mr. Gadd and my father's sister, Nora, were living with us. My father's mother had died some years earlier. Old Mr. Gadd went to live with Nora after she married. [Harry Wellstead started at Old Shoreham school in April 1923, and was then living at Old Erringham.]

Father worked on the railways with grandfather for a while after we left Old Erringham farm, about 1926. We lived in Beeding for a short time, then came to Gothic House, on Old Shoreham Road, in 1927, when I was coming up to 4 years old.

Gothic House was a railway inspector's home. When it became vacant my father applied for it and was very surprised when he got it. It seems no-one else wanted it. It is still owned by the railway company, which has changed its name several times. The railway arches were clear when we moved here, except the arch nearest the road, which was boarded across on the south side with a door. That was our way in.

Railway length man. Father worked on the railway from about 1925/6. He was a 'length man'. He worked on the railway line repairing the track and replacing sleepers etc. It was frequently foggy along the track by the river Adur and he then did 'fogging'. This involved placing a detonator on the track when the steam train was approaching a 'stop' signal. The explosion would warn the engine driver to stop. When the line was clear, the driver would be waved on by flag. All the railway workers had to be tested for colour blindness. My father transferred to the main line before 1939 and continued working on the railway until he died in 1944.

Walked to school. When I was at Old Shoreham school, I walked there via Freehold Street and the cinder path. I believe the Bypass Road was already there, but not as wide as it is now. I moved to Southwick school at age 11.

Mrs. Mary Sargent (nee Rothwell b. 1941) lived in a houseboat by the toll bridge and attended Old Shoreham school.

Our houseboat was berthed on the north side of Old Shoreham toll bridge, with the rear facing Steyning Road. It was moored in a channel, dug out of the bank, which is still there close to the bridge. Mother believes the channel was already there when we arrived. My older brother Robin [b.1940] started at Old Shoreham school on 24 October 1946, which must be when we moored there. Mother says we were there for about two years.

Hose pipe across railway line. Mrs. Fuller lived in the house nearest the toll bridge on the west side of Steyning Road [No. 1]. We ran a hose pipe across the railway line, between trains, from her tap to fill up our water tank.

Asked to move. The land belonged to the Duke of Norfolk and we were told to leave. Ours was the only houseboat by Old Shoreham bridge at that time. We moved up-river beyond the present fly-over, to the bend in the river just south of Erringham. We sometimes played in the corn field on the opposite side of Steyning Road. We made tunnels in the corn. The farmhouse looks out over the field and we were seen. The farmer, Mr. Strivens, came and told us off. We were there for about eight years.

No address. We never had an address. We used 447 Upper Shoreham Road, the Post Office, for our postal address. After we moved we still walked to school. We walked everywhere! I left Old Shoreham school in July 1952 to go to Southwick Secondary Modern school. We were still living on the houseboat near Erringham at that time.

Neil Rothwell was actually our step-father. We took his name and were always known as Rothwell. He and mother had more children together. He was a marine engineer and had a marine engine repair business in Southwick. He was a drinker. I do not know why he chose to live in Shoreham; I think he just liked the idea of being private and hard to find.

Converted lifeboat. The boat was a 35 foot converted lifeboat with a narrow beam, so did not give us much space. It had two rooms. The bedroom where Robin and I slept was at the front of the boat, facing across the river. The one main cabin was towards the back of the boat. From the bank you went through the door at the back of the boat, past two cupboards, into the cabin. On the right [starboard] side of the cabin there was a pull down bed which my mother and step-father slept in. When you pushed it back it made a settee. On the left side of the cabin was a black range with a chimney from the top, two seats, and a square hole with a lamp in it. That was a paraffin lamp, with a glass, which we lit at night. We obviously had no electricity.

At the front of the cabin was a narrow door, beyond which was a toilet on the left and a kitchen on the right. The kitchen was very small, no bigger than the toilet. The toilet was one where you put water in and pumped. You only ever pumped after high tide when the river had turned and was flowing out to sea. You went on through another narrow door into our small bedroom, at the front of the boat, where my brother and I slept in a big bed.

Six living on boat. When our two sisters came along, father extended the rear end of the boat, up and over the cockpit, to make an extra room. Robin had part of that with his own little kitchen, and I had a bunk along the other side. Our sisters had the front bedroom. It was all very cramped and we were still living in those conditions when I was sixteen. My mother was lovely. I do not know why she put up with it. It was dreadful, but I often walk along there and I wish I had a photograph of the houseboat.

Bus blown off bridge. When the bus was blown off the bridge [1949] we collected shoes and handbags washed up by the river. The police came and collected them. [On the evening of 1 January 1949, icy conditions and 80 m.p.h. winds caused a Southdown double decker bus, with 25 passengers, to skid off Old Shoreham bridge onto the river bank below. The bus rolled onto its side. Luckily it was low tide and no-one was killed. Mrs. Firthkettle of the Red Lion p.h. provided a ladder to help the passengers escape.]

Terrible storm. One night, when I was about age 12, there was a terrible storm [probably 1 January 1953]. The water whipped up very quickly and our boat was washed up onto the bank. Mother and we four children got off the boat and sheltered in a water tank which had been dumped on the bank. Dad got the lamp and a tarpaulin. When it calmed down we walked to the telephone box in the village. The police came and helped us and we spent the rest of the night in Shoreham. It was reported in the Shoreham Herald as an heroic rescue by the police, but it wasn't really like that. I remember one policeman had his hat blown into the river and had to wade in for it.

The Boxalls lived in the thatched cottage at the top of Connaught Avenue [No. 108, 1949 directory]. I used to play with their little girl. She had a pram and I did not. She ran out into the road one day, was run over by a lorry and lost her leg as a result. I was probably about 7 years old then [c.1948]. I also played with the Tuppens.

Free coal. The engine drivers on the Steyning line sometimes threw great lumps of coal from the train for us as they passed. They usually gave a toot-toot as they approached. I have no idea how it started. The lumps were so big that we had to break them up so that we could carry the coal.

Mr. Northeast. When we were living up the river, near Erringham, Mr. Northeast was already living on a houseboat opposite us, on the west side of the river, at the bottom of Coombes. He had a long thin shed at the back of his boat, like an allotment shed, which was their toilet. When it blew away during a storm he was very upset. We left there when I was about 16 [1957] and moved into Shoreham. Some time after that I saw Mr. Northeast's boat moored by the Old Shoreham toll bridge. He was there for some years. He was a character

Mrs. Nellie Alexander (nee Snook b.1915) lived on Buckingham Street and attended Old Shoreham school. Her mother went to the original school c.1892.

Father killed in war. My father, Alfred George Snook, came from Wiltshire with two of his brothers. I believe they worked on the farm for a while. Father was killed in the first world war and mother later re-married to Walter Bowyer. Alf Bowyer is my step-brother. We were living at No. 1 Buckingham Street by 1919, when our older brother Frank (b. 1913) started at Old Shoreham school. We lived there until we moved to Eastern Avenue in 1933. Our house, the first on the right, was practically on the railway bank. There were two terraces of houses on our side. The access to Buckingham Place & Buckingham Cottages was between the terraces. All the houses were demolished in the 1950's and replaced by flats.

Ran the Sussex Pad. Our mother was Helen Frances, nee Smart. The Smarts are an Old Shoreham family. Her father was a publican. Mother was the youngest and was born at the Steam Packet p.h. at Littlehampton. At one stage they ran the old Sussex Pad at Lancing and mother walked across the toll bridge to Old Shoreham school [see photo 65]. We have a postcard of the old Sussex Pad which has F. Smart on the sign board. The Sussex Pad burned down in 1905, but they had already moved to Old Shoreham by then.

Grocery shop. After the Sussex Pad, mum lived at No. 23* Old Shoreham; the westerly one of three cottages which are now the Amsterdam p.h. It had a large rear garden and a grocery shop by the side. [F. Smart, grocer, is listed at Old Shoreham in 1901.] The road was then just a narrow lane in front of the cottages, and they had a small holding on the opposite [north] side of the lane. The western part of the present Upper Shoreham Road was built through the small holding [c.1928]. Mum worked in the shop and drove the pony and trap to Steyning market with the produce from the small holding. The pony and trap were kept in a barn on the west side of the house. When we were out for walks, our older sister Florence [b. 1902] would point to the attic window on the west side of No. 23 and say 'I was born up there!' [see photo 10]. [*The inter-war village numbering system.]

School photo c.1892. Mother died in September 1946 aged nearly 62, so was born c.1884. She went to the original Old Shoreham school, the one which still stands, and we have a photo of her taken there at age 7 or 8. Our oldest sister, Florence, born in 1902, also went to the old school. The later school, which we younger children attended, was demolished and replaced by St. Nicolas Court. [Florence started at the school in March 1908. The later school opened in 1914 and closed in 1971.]

A long walk for some. There was a Puckett family at Applesham, on the way to Coombes. The children had to walk to Old Shoreham, but were later [1927] transferred to Steyning school and went by school bus. [The Puckett children from Applesham entered the school as follows: William (1913), Dorothy (1916), John (1918), Mary (1921), Arthur (1922), Herbert 1926).]

Buckingham park became public. I started at Old Shoreham school in 1922 and stayed there until I turned 14. We walked to school either along what is now Connaught Avenue, or along Old Shoreham Road and across Charlie Miller's field. We occasionally came back past what is now the Amsterdam p.h. There was a ramshackle tin building opposite there [west side - see photo 68]. Around 1930 they started building houses along the east side of Old Shoreham Road, on the orchard which went through to Connaught Avenue. When I was 12 years old [1931], Buckingham Park, previously a private park, became public and we started having school football matches there.

Squire Bridger's funeral. Squire Bridger [Lt. Col. H. C. Bridger], who lived at Adur Lodge, died whilst I was at school [c.1929]. We children had to line the path through the church yard whilst the coffin was carried through to St. Nicolas church. The tomb by the north east corner of the church was opened up for his coffin. Some of the boys dared one another to climb down into it, but I did not see anyone do it. Squire Bridger took an interest in the community. His two elderly spinster sisters [Dulcibella & Florence] were governors of Old Shoreham school. They sometimes wandered around the classrooms inspecting our work. I can remember a group of us carol singing outside Adur Lodge and being invited in for mince pies.

Stood up and was killed. Our house, No. 1 Buckingham Street, was the nearest to Old Shoreham Road, and very close to the railway bridge for the Steyning line. That bridge [removed c.1991] was lower than the one for the coastal railway line and there were some accidents as a result. In the early days, the buses had an open top. When they approached the bridges, the conductor had to shout to the passengers to stay sitting. I witnessed an accident when one man stood up and was killed by the Steyning line bridge. He had stood up after the first bridge. He was lying on the ground with his head almost severed. I had to put it out of my mind. These days you would be offered counselling if you witnessed something like that.

Bus stuck under bridge. The first double decker bus got stuck under the Steyning line bridge. They had to let the tyres down to get it out. I imagine they lowered the road after that. On another occasion one of the local lads with a bicycle showed the driver of a large vehicle how to avoid the bridge by going over the level crossing.

Red Lion. In the late 1930's we did a lot of our courting at the Red Lion, which had a number of tiny rooms. One room had just a seat against the wall and a shelf in front of you on the opposite wall where you could stand your drink. That was it! It was really no more than a piece of passage. That was at the front of the pub, where you go down some steps. The Red Lion was a fascinating little place [see photo 66].

Connaught Avenue. We married in 1934 and came to live in Connaught Avenue. Ours was the first bungalow to be built south of Colvill Avenue. There were already some bungalows further north. Before those bungalows were built, there was a stile at the bend and a footpath through Charlie Miller's field to Old Shoreham Road. [The stile/gate is shown in photo 15.] By the time we moved here it had become the twitten which goes between Nos. 174 & 176 Old Shoreham Road.

Elm trees. There was no road below Colvill Avenue in 1934, it was like a narrow cart track. North of Colvill Avenue it widened out and there were elm trees in the middle, up to the bend. You could walk either side of them. The trees were felled when the road was made up. As children, we knew the track as the cinder path. There were orchards on the south west side of the cinder path, and a corn field on the other side. [The corn field became the grammar school playing field from c.1927.]

Blackout. The road was made up in 1939, with footpaths and lamp posts. I remember it well because our son Malcolm was born in the February and the doctor didn't like having to get through the road works. Then the war came and the blackout stopped the street lamps being used.

Swiss Gardens. The lower end of the cinder path, between Freehold Street and Victoria Road, was called the dungeons. That was a concrete tunnel which was a remnant of the path through the old Swiss Gardens. Most of the buildings which belonged to the old Swiss Gardens were where the school now stands. My mother-in-law went dancing at the ballroom when she was a young woman.

Sunday school treats. I remember the row of elm trees to which Dorothy Lillywhite refers [p.16]. When I was very young we had Sunday school treats in that field, which was to the east of the school. That was before the concrete road was built. [The concrete road was Bypass Road, built c.1928, now the western end of Upper Shoreham Road.]

Colvill Avenue. When we moved here [1934] the terrace of houses on Colvill Avenue was already built, but not the bungalows. [The 1933 map does not show Colvill Avenue.] There was a footpath from the end of Colvill Avenue, past the electricity sub-station, to the concrete road [Upper Shoreham Road]. We went that way to visit relations. It came out by the Adur Stores [417 Upper Shoreham Road] but was later blocked off.

Perryman's shop. I got to know Win Perryman through calling at the shop after we moved here [see photos 74R & 75]. She played tennis in Brighton and I went with her to watch. We took her to a dance, where she met Jack Cotman and they eventually married [1942]. She later asked me to look after the shop while they took a holiday. After that I worked at the shop all day on Fridays and Saturdays. They were the busy days for the shop.

Perryman's was a grocery shop with a lot of land [about 3/4 acre]. The land is now occupied by Tollgate House and the two adjacent houses. Much of it was orchard. Fruit and vegetables from the garden were sold in the shop. Win sold groceries, bacon, eggs, cheese, cakes and some sweets, which were kept in jars. She did not sell hardware, fuel, candles or cigarettes.

As you went into the shop the counter was on the right hand side. There was a sitting room on the left. Behind the sitting room was a large scullery and behind the shop was another room where the bacon was sliced on the machine.

Little stock. Win didn't keep a big stock of anything because there wasn't much room for storage. Some stock, such as potatoes, was stored in the building at the back, which they always called the bakehouse. They had a big freezer where Win kept the perishables, but it made a lot of noise and annoyed Mr. Perryman at night. That was in the scullery. That had a big wooden table which was scrubbed each evening after the shop closed, a large shallow sink, and a shelf along the wall. The scales for weighing the potatoes were kept in there; the type with a bowl. A wholesaler delivered each week, but Win only carried a small stock; perhaps a dozen tins of beans.

Credit. Customers wanting credit usually said: 'Would you book it to me please?' A few of them had their own book into which which they wrote their order. The customer was expected to pay at the end of the week, with the main grocery order. Some made excuses about having other bills to pay, and there were a few who got weeks behind. Win was too easy going with them.

Win delivered to a few customers on Upper Shoreham Road and Connaught Avenue, but most people came into the shop. She delivered on Saturdays on a bicycle with a front carrier. I delivered on it when she couldn't.

Mr. Perryman. Win's father had retired from the Metropolitan Police and often told us stories about those days. When he was on duty at the House of Commons he used to have to shout 'Who goes home?'. He was a very kind and interesting man. I didn't get to know Mrs. Perryman. She was senile and often put things where they couldn't be found.

The shop opened about 9 a.m. on the days I worked there [Fridays & Saturdays] and stayed open until about 8 p.m. We did not close for lunch, so it was a very long day. At that time Win was married and living on Connaught Avenue.

Lovely cup of tea. Mr. Perryman always made us a pot of tea, which he served in the sitting room. He made a lovely cup of tea; the best I have ever tasted. He made the tea and took it into the sitting room. He also took the kettle, which he stood in the fireplace. Before he poured the tea he would fill each cup with hot water to warm it up, then tip it out and pour the tea. He always followed the same ritual. When I first knew them they served teas in the front garden.

Perryman's shop

Mrs. Connie Perryman (b.1920) married Winifred Perryman's brother Bert and helped in Perryman's grocery shop, previously a bakery for 60 years.

London policeman. Mr. Charles Perryman [b.1873] was a City of London policeman. He was christened Albert Charles, but his wife, Flo, always called him 'Charl'. I married their son, Bert, who was also christened Albert Charles. During his time with the Metropolitan Police, Mr. Perryman did guard duty at the House of Commons, Buckingham Palace and No. 10 Downing Street.

Retired in 1921. Mr. Perryman's retirement certificate says that he served from June 1896 to September 1921; when he was age 48. He met his wife Florence, who was a cook, during that period. Their first child, Ivan, died as a baby. Winifred was born in 1910 and Bert, my late husband, in 1912. When Mr. Perryman retired they had to vacate their police flat in Westminster. They moved to Haywards Heath for a couple of years. Mr. Perryman worked as a coalman then, but cycled around Sussex looking for a place to settle.

They moved to Old Shoreham in 1923, taking over from Mr. Bullock [listed as a baker in 1923]. Mr. Perryman ran the premises as a general shop, and grew produce on the land. Mrs. Perryman, who he called 'Missus', had developed Alzheimers disease, though it wasn't named then, and was unable to run the shop. She was not involved with the shop when I first knew her [1937]. She died in the early 1950's.

Win ran the shop. Win and her father delivered groceries by bicycle. I helped Win in the shop before the war. When we came down [from Slough] during the war I helped her with the ration coupons and the books. Win was a very helpful and friendly person [see photo 74R]. You could always knock on the door after the shop was closed if you needed something urgently, such as an aspirin. The shop took up most of her time.

The shop. The sitting room occupied the front part of what was probably the original building, under the thatched roof. The Perrymans served teas in there in the early days [see illus. 75]. The shop was on the west side of the cottage, under the low roof. There was a room behind the shop, separated by a wooden partition with a window in it. They ate their meals in there and could see through the window if anyone came into the shop. That room also had a window [west side] which looked over next door's garden. The room had a range, against the rear wall of the cottage, where they sometimes made toast, but the cooking was done on the gas stove in the scullery, which was behind the sitting room. The stock for the shop was kept everywhere. Electricity was put into the cottage after the war, but the old gas mantles were still there when they left the property.

The scullery had a flag stone floor but it was uneven and dangerous. Mr. Perryman had it cemented over. It had a small porcelain sink with a cold tap above, on the wall, and there was a big gas cooker and a table. There were two big cupboards, mainly used for storing stock for the shop. There was a door from the scullery, through the east wall, into the garden.

The bathroom was downstairs, within the main walls of the cottage. It had previously been a cold store. It had a stone floor, a cast iron bath, a gas boiler, and a flushing toilet. There was a cess pit near the garage.

Two bedrooms. The stairs were at the back of the cottage. The stairs turned and came up to quite a large landing where there was a spare bed, used as a guest bed. From the landing there were two doors, one into the main [front] bedroom, above the sitting room, and the other into a smaller bedroom above the scullery & bathroom. There was a fireplace in the north wall of the front bedroom. I remember making a fire in there when Mr. Perryman was old and not feeling too well. It was a large room.

Old bakehouse. The building behind the cottage [see illus. 75] was the old bakehouse, which was nearly as big as the cottage. The ovens were still in there. They were quite large and low down, just above the floor. A child could have easily climbed in there.

The tea garden probably developed in the 1920's from making sandwiches for workers from Ricardo's. Teas were served in the sitting room, and outside on the front lawn in good weather. It only lasted until the war. A Jewish gentleman from Hove frequently came over on his pony and trap for evening tea.

On the book. Win was very helpful and friendly, and some took advantage. Money was short in those days and everything was 'on the book'. That is, people would go in for provisions on the understanding that they would pay at the weekend. Sometimes things didn't get entered in the book because the shop was busy, and when people didn't pay on time she wouldn't press them.

Reception at Old Shoreham school. Win married Jack Cotman, a widower, in 1942. They were married at St. Mary's church in June and held their reception at the school on St. Nicolas Lane. Afterwards, they lived at Jack's house, No. 5 Connaught Avenue. Their only child, Rhona, was born in July 1944. I can remember us loading provisions into Rhona's pram and taking it to farmer Nye at Little Buckingham farm. Win died a couple of years ago. She was always out on her bicycle, and was well known and liked.

Coffin carried to church. In the latter days the shop wasn't paying and Win wanted to sell it, but Mr. Perryman liked his independence and wanted to carry on living there. Win worked at the shop during the day, and her father came to us alternately for Sunday lunch. He died at home, age 87, in January 1960. [A report in the Herald of 22 January 1960 says that he knew four prime ministers during his time with the Metropolitan Police, and that he was a keen cricketer who played for the police at Lords and the Oval.] We walked with the coffin from the shop, past the Red Lion, to the church yard. The shop was under threat from road proposals and was later purchased by the Council.

Picked mushrooms. I missed Mr. Perryman as much as my own father. He was a man you could really talk to. In my courting days I often went for a walk on the hills with him and the dog, named Tug, whilst Bert was tuning his motor cycles in the garage. There was a footpath opposite [east of] what is now the lower car park on Mill Hill. We picked mushrooms along there, but later the ground was ploughed up.

Snooker club. Mr. Perryman ran a snooker and darts club on St. Nicolas Lane soon after he moved to Old Shoreham. It was in the old building that was just to the west of Old Shoreham garage [see photo 19]. I believe it was just a club, not a business. He probably missed that sort of thing after leaving the police force. [The building became Adur Cafe, then a Post Office, see below.]

Adur Cafe. [The 1923 directory lists the building, photo 19, as the Adur Cafe, run by A. W. Bulloch. The 1926 directory lists it as the Adur Cafe, run by Miss G. McIlroy. The 1930 directory lists it as the Adur Cafe, run by Miss Bates. The 1933 map shows the building as a Post Office. The 1934 directory lists it as Old Shoreham Post Office, run by Miss B. C. Bates.]

Bert Perryman (b.1912)

Shed on Connaught Avenue. I started going with Bert when I was 17 [1937]. The lane at the top of Connaught Avenue was quite narrow then, with a hedge along the west side. The Perrymans had a shed which opened onto the lane. When they put in the footpaths, before the war, the hedge was taken away and the shed was moved nearer the cottage. They put a concrete drive-in between the road and the shed. I believe the hedge was on a bank. A wooden fence was put between the pavement and the garden.

Railway enthusiast. Bert had a model steam engine as a child, and a track layout on the upper floor of the shed. He served an apprenticeship at the Brighton railway works but was laid off because of the depression. Later, he built working model steam engines and wrote a number of books.

Motor cycle accident. Bert had his first car when he was 14 [c.1926]. That was a Fiat, formerly an undertakers car. He had an accident on his motor cycle when he was 17, along The Street. He was hit by a car coming from the Red Lion. He nearly lost a leg. One leg ended up two inches shorter, but he was able to take up motor cycle racing. He won a Gold Star at Brooklands. During the war he installed and maintained large American machines at Langley Alloys in Slough. Afterwards, he worked for Miles at Shoreham airport.

Taxi service. Bert became ill through working with asbestos during his apprenticeship. He always felt better outside and liked driving, so we started a taxi business. We ran it from our home in Adur Avenue, but had a sign at the shop.

[Mrs. Connie Perryman's maternal grandfather was Sidney Chewter, who lived at 139 Old Shoreham Road between 1914 & 1945.]

Perryman's shop

Mrs. Rhona Jenner (nee Cotman, b.1944) is the daughter of Winifred Perryman, who ran Perryman's shop for over 30 years.

I can remember my mother saying what hard work shop keeping was in those days. Nothing was pre-packed. The cheese came whole and had to be cut with cheese wire. The bacon came as a side and had to be boned and sliced. One of mother's favourite tales was of how she boned a side of bacon the night before I was born; which was at 7.30 in the morning. Mother ran the business. She dealt with the money, the points from rationing, and the ordering in addition to serving in the shop. She also had three elderly people to keep an eye on, and a small child in tow. [Rationing of clothes & sweets ceased in 1949. Rationing finally ended in July 1954, after 14 years, when meat rationing ceased.]

The scullery had an enormous table in the centre. In the summer there was a long sticky fly-paper suspended from the beams. The cat usually slept in the scullery; hygiene regulations weren't the same then.

The garden was a wonderful place for children, with lots of secret hidey-holes. I frequently played there with my cousins Christopher and Ivan. When we were bored with it, grandfather would take us up onto Mill Hill, 'Grandad's hills' to us. He put apples in his pockets and always took us to the same stile, where he smoked his pipe and we had our apples. He would tell us stories, or tell us about the countryside.

The shop was always open until 8 p.m. on Fridays whilst mother made up orders for the weekend. She would always try to help out if anyone needed something as an emergency. I can remember my father getting angry when someone knocked on our door at 5 Connaught Avenue one Christmas morning because they had run out of toilet rolls.

Mother was a very enthusiastic member of the Townswomen's Guild, along with her friend Doris Gilbert. Their refreshments for the meetings were legendary. Mother was a very good tennis player in her youth, and enjoyed watching the game all her life. Her other hobby was playing whist.

Father was an enthusiastic member of the Rowing Club and took part in many regattas. He worked for Godsmark & Co. His mother ran the East Street Arms at one time.

Mr. Christopher Perryman (b.1947), son of Bert Perryman, often visited Perryman's shop to see his grandfather and his aunt Winifred.

The cottage had stone floors throughout. Grandfather's sitting room was at the front of the cottage, which faces north. It had a fireplace on the north side, a window on the east side, and a low wooden panelled ceiling. The old gas light fittings were still there. There was a piano in there, and grandfather's arm chair. As you went into the shop, the sitting room was to the left [east]. The scullery was behind the sitting room, and there was a bathroom in the south-east corner, off the scullery.

The shop window was just a display area. As you went into the shop, there were some steps down and a high counter on the right hand side, about 4 feet high, which ran from the doorway towards the rear. When the doors were shut you were effectively standing in a long corridor. The till was at the far end of the counter. I remember storage jars, bacon slicers, and an old table. Large tins of biscuits were stacked on the left, opposite the counter. That part had a floor made of large quarry tiles, and it dipped in the middle due to wear. The tiles were a dark red. Aunt Win often had to go out the back to get what the customer wanted. There was always a big block of cheese in the scullery, and a side of bacon. There were two bacon slicers and several scales. It was a busy shop, and a focal point for the village.

The old bakehouse was a separate building adjacent to the cottage, with a yard between. Grandfather kept produce and chicken feed in there, and the rabbits. It had a large door and lots of beams inside with hooks. There was an old mangle in there and various old appliances. I remember he hung a pot of ale on one of the hooks. It was a big brown bottle with a screw top. He hung it there to keep it cool and would pour a little from it each day.

Outside, there was a path along the east side of the cottage, between the cottage and the front lawn. There was a chestnut tree. Behind the cottage was a very large galvanised tank, about 6 x 4 feet and about 4 feet high, which collected rain water. Grandfather always brought in water from that tank for washing and shaving because he said it was better than tap water.

Garden & orchard. Grandfather grew produce in the large garden. There were chicken runs, fruit trees, areas for growing vegetables, and an air raid shelter. Tomatoes were grown alongside the garage. The chicken droppings were put into a large earthenware vat with rain water. It was eventually used as fertiliser. Grandfather grew large tomatoes and enormous rhubarb. We children cut the tops off the rhubarb and wore them as hats. The garden was a marvellous place to play.

End of an era. Aunt Win was running the shop when [1958] plans were announced to put a concrete fly-over through the village. The shop was subsequently purchased by the Council, after grandfather died, and remained empty for a number of years.

The Bishop family lived at 6 The Street for over 40 years. Mr. Bishop was foreman at Ayling's market garden. Their older son, Bert, died in the 1914-18 war as a young man. Mrs. Dora Bishop, wife of younger son 'Jim' Bishop says:

Bishops and Dukes. My husband, Stanley James Bishop, was born in August 1917 and died in January 1995. He preferred to be called Jim. His parents married in 1896 at Old Shoreham church. They were William Bishop age 21 from New Shoreham and Ellen Duke age 18 from Old Shoreham [marriage certificate]. Her father, James Duke, is the man on the left in the toll bridge photo [photo 3]. From family postcards, the Dukes lived at 27 Bridge Cottages, Old Shoreham in 1906, then at 4 The Street in 1915. [In 1891, James Duke, age 46, a gardener, was living at Prospect Place, now No. 11 The Street.]

Bridge cottages. [The 1903 directory lists F. Smart, grocer, at No. 26 and James Duke at No. 27. F. Smart operated from one of three cottages which are now the Amsterdam - see p. 85 - later known as No. 23 Old Shoreham. From this, it appears that Bridge Cottages were the pair of cottages on Steyning Road which face directly across Old Shoreham bridge, now Nos. 2 & 4 Steyning Road, but numbered 24 & 25 Old Shoreham after the first war.]

Lived there 43 years. [At a Ministry of Health Inquiry, in January 1939, into the proposed demolition of No. 6 The Street, it was stated that Mr. W. J. G. Bishop had lived there for 43 years. The cottage was demolished in 1946.]

Royal Sussex Cycle Battalion. Jim's father, William, was foreman at Aylings market garden on Kingston Lane. Jim's older brother Herbert G. Bishop, known as Bert, delivered for International Stores on a bicycle after he left school. Bert joined the Royal Sussex Regiment and was killed in the 1914-18 war [see memorial list on page 125]. He was in the cycle battalion. We have a postcard sent to him in August 1916 addressed to Pte H. G. Bishop, No. 2422, 3/6 Cycle Batt. Royal Sussex Regiment, A. lines, B Coy, 31 Hut, Purfleet Camp, Essex. [The 6th (Cyclist) Battalion of the Royal Sussex Regiment was raised at Brighton in 1912. The 3rd/6th was raised at Brighton in May 1915.]

Jim repaired cycles. Jim was born in August 1917. He went to Old Shoreham school, and left at age 14 in 1931 to work at Gammans on the corner of Gordon Road [described as the Cycle Works in the school register]. Neither Bert nor Jim had children to continue the line.

Jim was in the R.A.F. during the second world war. He was stationed at Upper Heyford in Oxfordshire when the bomber crashed at Coombes. He wrote to say he knew all about it as it was one from their own aerodrome. He thought he might be sent down to the crash, but Ford aerodrome had cleared the wreckage. The letter says he spent his spare time making model aeroplanes and had nearly completed a Spitfire and a Beaufighter. He was with 89 Squadron in India in 1944. Jim later worked for Tates garage and Bowthorpe, the electrical engineers of Southwick. He was keen on aeroplanes and spent a lot of time at Shoreham airport.

Lesser Foxholes

Mr. Christopher Rawlings was born in 1939 at Lesser Foxholes, The Street, and attended Lancing College.

Father, John Herbert Rawlings, was born in London in 1910. He was always known as Jack. His father started a very successful electrical engineering business, Avo Ltd., in London in the 1920's. Father went to Brighton College. He left school at age 16 and trained as an electrical engineer. Our parents married in 1935, by which time father was running Avo Ltd. with his father. Mother, Edith Valerie (nee Windle), was born in 1911 at Croydon and was from a cultured background. She was known as Valerie. She was very studious and won a place at Oxford University; quite unusual for a girl at that time. She did not take it up because her mother died and she was needed at home.

Sussex Shipbuilding Co. After marrying, our parents lived in London for a short time, then moved down to Lesser Foxholes in late 1937. Just before moving to Shoreham, father had an ocean racer built at the Sussex Shipbuilding Co. on Shoreham Beach. She was launched in 1936 and called Erivale, which is an anagram of Valerie. Father must have liked the product because he bought the company, but we are not sure when. He was obviously fascinated by ships and the sea and I believe that is why my parents moved to Shoreham. I remember going to Sussex Shipbuilding as a child and seeing lifeboats. I believe they built landing craft during the war. Father still ran the electrical business in London. [Sussex Shipbuilding is shown on the 1930 map. It changed hands & name several times. Latterly it was known as Watercraft. The site is now the Emerald Quay housing development.]

Ocean racer. In 1949 father built an ocean racing yacht called Gulvain. That was an innovative light displacement design by J. Laurent Giles, with a 55 foot hull made from 'Birmabright' aluminium alloy, and an alloy mast. She was first to finish in the Cowes-Dinard race of July 1949. In 1950 the Americans paid for Gulvain to be shipped over to Newport. The crew of 6 or 8 raced her to Bermuda, when she came 9th. Gulvain then took part in the 3000 mile Bermuda to Plymouth race of 1950, and won. She was skippered by Capt. Humphrey Barton and did the journey in 18 days, three days ahead of the rest of the fleet. However, Gulvain was larger than the other competitors and was handicapped down to fourth place. It was a tough journey, with 5 days and nights of storm. Father often recalled harrowing incidents on the voyage. I believe the novelty of racing had worn off, and father sold the yacht in 1951. Gulvain was re-fitted in 1990/1 and has won races since.

Father enjoyed his life; he worked hard but also lived it up a bit. He enjoyed yachting, and often went shooting at Arundel & Winchester.

Lesser Foxholes had been recently built when our parents moved to Old Shoreham in 1937 [see photo 76]. I believe they purchased the adjoining field at the same time. In our time, the garden was about 2½ acres and the paddock a further 2 acres. [Shown on the 1933 map as 1 acre, with a 3½ acre field to the north]. The house still stands [now called Foxholes Lodge] but the garden became the development known as Lesser Foxholes, built in the late 1960's. The house had a small entrance hall on the east side and a large central dining area which looked across the river Adur. There was a sitting room on the south side of the dining area, and a playroom/nursery on the north side of it, again facing west. There was a modest kitchen. Upstairs was a main bedroom and, I believe, seven other bedrooms; two of them added, above the dining area, after my parents bought the property. There was just one small bathroom. Central heating was installed in the 1950's. Before that we had coal fires, plus electric bar fires in some of the bedrooms. It was very cold in the winter but you just accepted it.

As children we spent most of our time in the playroom/nursery. Shortly after the war started my parents had a dug-out air raid shelter constructed alongside [west of] the playroom, and there were stairs down into it. We used it whenever there was a threat of bombing.

Children & schools.   Nigel was born in 1935, Diana in 1938, myself in 1939, Richard in 1941, and Peter in 1944 [see photo 78L]. We started school at Greenfields, which was on the east side of Buckingham park. It was about three quarters of the way up Parkside, on the west side, and was run by Miss Pascoe. I used to walk there along the Upper Shoreham Road. I believe it was a large bungalow and that there were perhaps 20 or more children attending. We spent a year there. At lunch times we would go off in a 'crocodile' to the little cafe in Buckingham park. It was a good little school and I have happy memories of it.

After Greenfields, at about 6 years old, I went to Broadwater pre-prep. school by the Thomas A' Becket p.h. in Worthing. There again we were marched off at lunch time to the Thomas A' Becket, where we all sat around a big table with the head teacher, Miss Kay, who drank half a pint of stout. She was a formidable character. After that, at age 8, I went to Broadwater Manor school at Broadwater. That was quite a tough prep. school.

Soon after starting at Broadwater Manor school, I often cycled there and back each day; a distance of more than 4 miles. Sometimes mother would take me and my bicycle by car in the morning, and I would cycle back. You could not let a child do that these days because of the traffic. Life was harder in those days, and there was petrol rationing. Sometimes I went by train and walked from Worthing station.

My brothers and I went to Lancing College, as boarders, from age 13. That was also a tough school and I felt the standard of teaching was poor. I learned nothing in the first year, and I did not like the school. That was a long time ago, of course. Our sister Diana went to the Warren school in Worthing for a while, then went to school in Bexhill.

Sister Wadey, a splendid professional nurse, came and took over for the first month or two after each of us was born. She then moved on to another assignment. She was not local because she was involved with Nigel's birth in London before the family came to Shoreham.

Nanny Chandler was, and is, a lovely person who lived with us from 1939 to 1946 and was very much in charge of us. We had to be good-mannered at the table and were never allowed to leave anything. It was wartime and food was generally scarce. A number of other people worked in the house, but mostly part-time.

Nanny Chandler took us for long walks to keep us fit and healthy. You could walk anywhere in those days. Unknown to us at the time, she had fallen in love with Dick Passmore, who has the farm at Coombes. We were frequently taken for walks in that direction, via the toll bridge, and they would meet. Eventually we realised! I often cycled over to Coombes to visit her after she left to get married in 1946 [now Mrs. Mary Passmore]. We then had a succession of au-pair girls, who lived-in, plus the local part-time ladies, such as Ivy Bradford, sister of Fred Tester, the gardener.

George Bartlett looked after the garden during the war. He had retired as signal man at Old Shoreham bridge, and always smoked a pipe. The $2^1/_2$ acre garden took a lot of looking after, and was a full time job. The mowing took a day, and there was a large vegetable garden and orchards, herbaceous borders and the ponds. He became ill and could not continue.

Fred Tester returned to us as gardener in 1946, after his time in the R.A.F. He was always a very nice, helpful and patient man. I cannot recall him ever losing his temper. I believe Fred was not an experienced gardener when he first came to work for my parents. Mother probably taught him quite a lot. Looking after the garden was his prime task.

Mother organised the house, kept household accounts and was very meticulous. There was obviously a lot involved in running a large house and grounds and five children. It was well organised. We had set times for meals, for example, when we all sat round the table. As children, we all had our little tasks to do, such as helping with the washing-up. We were not spoilt in any way. Mother regularly drove the car before she became very ill in the 1950's. Fred Tester took over part of the running of the house for a while at that time.

When our shoes needed repairing, mother would take them to a shop called Watts in Worthing. After repair, the shoes were put in a box and sent back by bus to the Red Lion, where they were picked up by arrangement. The quality of service in those days was excellent. Mother would phone Eade's Stores on Brunswick Road and order everything she needed. It was delivered to the house by car.

Skilled riders. We had two ponies to start with, both fairly ordinary. Nigel & Diana were particularly keen on riding and acquired better horses, but I did not enjoy riding. I remember when I was about 8 years old my horse bolted at a gymkhana at Small Dole. Nigel chased after us and grabbed the bit, rather like something out of a cowboy movie. That stopped the horse rapidly and I flew off. That put me off riding. Nigel & Diana were quite fearless and became very good riders. Nigel, who is no longer alive, was particularly good. He competed at White City, hunted, and later, when he was in Rhodesia, took up polo. Richard and Peter were also excellent equestrians and fine tennis players.

Church was obligatory for us children on a Sunday, and St. Nicolas church was a great meeting place for the village. We went to Sunday school every week before we started at Lancing College, and there would be 20 or 30 children and one or both of their parents. The Rev. Percy Shelley was a lovely man who really liked children and he made a great impression on me. He seemed like a saint to me. I believe we were all in the choir at some stage, and each week one of the children would be selected to give a reading.

Apart from Sunday school, I do not recall us mixing much with other village children, though we have photographs taken with some, such as Hazel Frampton. I have very happy memories of childhood at Lesser Foxholes. We were a united family and we were particularly close to mother, who was a wonderful woman.

The garden was practically bare in February 1938, just a path and grass, with the field to the north. The garden was laid out and planted in spring 1938. The drive was put in during the summer of 1938. There were two large ponds. Water flowed from the top pond, on the east side of the garden, near The Street, to the lower (west) pond near the house [see photo 77]. There were several smaller ponds between, and a waterfall. The water was pumped back to the east pond through an underground pipe. We had a wicker fence between the garden & the field, with a stile to go over. The vegetable garden was over near Adur Cottage, where Mrs. House lived. She was a local school teacher and mother was quite friendly with her. We had a gate in the fence so that we could visit her easily.

The village. I remember well the farm and the thatched cottages on The Street. We hardly knew the people at Greystones, and I have no memory of children being there. Mrs. Daynes lived in one of the thatched cottages [No. 8, now Hunters Moon]. She was a delightful lady and I often did errands for her. The Divers lived next door at Brooking. Mr. Divers had been a school teacher in China, and his wife was Chinese.

Plenty to do. We rarely went away for holidays, but we had everything we wanted at Shoreham; the garden; the horses; the tennis courts; the downs; the river; and the beach, which we visited frequently after the war. During the war we swam in the river at Old Shoreham, to the north of the toll bridge. We all had bicycles and cycled around the area. We probably read quite a lot because we had no television until the Coronation in 1953.

Mother left Lesser Foxholes about 1966, largely because she knew the Shoreham by-pass would ruin the view from the house of the Adur valley.

Lesser Foxholes during the war

Mrs. Mary Passmore (nee Chandler b.1920) was nanny to the Rawlings children during the war.

Trained as nursery nurse. Having completed my nursery nurses training at St. Christopher's in Tunbridge Wells, I returned to Shoreham to join the Rawlings family at Lesser Foxholes shortly after the outbreak of war in 1939. I remained there as the children's nanny until I married in 1946.

House staff. Nigel was then 3½, Diana 20 months, and Christopher had just been born. Sister Wadey, who attended the birth of all the children, was still living-in. There was a residential cook, Nina. Gladys Stoner, the parlour maid, and Evelyn, who cleaned silver and did odd jobs, came in daily. They both lived close by. Fred Tester looked after the garden and heavy jobs outside, including the car.

Wartime staff shortage. Jack & Valerie Rawlings were such nice people to live with. They both worked very hard. Having been used to living up to a high standard, they found it very hard to see the staff leave one by one, but fully appreciated the war effort. Fred Tester joined the R.A.F., Gladys the A.T.S., etc., until we were left with just one part-time helper indoors. George Bartlett, after he retired as signalman & toll collector at Old Shoreham bridge, came to help in the garden, mainly growing vegetables and keeping an eye on the children when they rushed around the garden on their tricycles and bicycles and later ponies.

It was a great joy when Ivy Bradford, Fred Tester's sister, came to join us as a daily help. She lent a hand to anything and continued long after I left. Her brother Fred returned after being de-mobilised.

Long hours. Nursery nurses were expected to sleep with their charges and work all day. I came off duty at 7 p.m. I had half a day a week and one weekend a month off, and one weeks holiday a year. I should have had two hours off a day, but that was not possible during the war. In a reserved occupation you were expected to put in as much time as possible with the voluntary services, and, of course, everyone was pleased to do this. Mrs. Rawlings was very co-operative and I joined the Red Cross. We had to do a minimum of 50 hours in hospital (cycling to Worthing in my case) and keep up our exams and standards. We met and trained at Dobson's butchers shop, at the rear of St. Mary's Hall, as Lilian & Margaret Dobson were also nurses.

The wartime canteen. Our duties also involved helping at the little canteen on St. Nicolas Lane, next to the garden of the farm house [see photo 19]. I think we were in more danger of the roof falling in than a bomb hitting us. That was staffed mainly for the odd cup of tea for an air raid warden. Paul Plumb (who ran the gentlemen's outfitters in the High Street) was an errand boy in those days and frequently turned up for a cup of tea and bun for one warden or another, and always one for himself. There was always a good spirit in those those days. Fortunately Shoreham did not suffer a lot of casualties during the war, so our skills were not put to the test, but the motto was 'Be prepared'.

Air raids. I wore our college uniform all through the war. Life in the nursery was very disciplined, but we tried to make life fun for the children and they were lucky to have their mother's back up for their sport and education. We spent a lot of time out of doors. Air raids happened mainly at night and a dug-out shelter was made leading out of the nursery. When air raids were imminent we slept down there.

Evacuated. When Richard and Peter were born in 1941 & 1944, I was evacuated to Worcestershire with the older children, to stay with Mrs. Rawling's father, while sister Wadey came for 6 weeks to help deliver the new baby.

Petrol was rationed so we had to walk with the children to their first school at Greenfields in Parkside, pushing the younger ones in a large coach built pram across Buckingham park. If an air raid siren went off, we would head for the nearest shelter and wait for the all clear.

Good spirit. Although the war years were so terrible in many ways, there was a wonderful spirit of helpfulness and the streets during blackout hours were remarkably safe, with air raid wardens and other personnel about, and the military police.

Walks on the hills. We often went for long walks up Mill Hill. It was hard work pushing the pram up, but easier coming home. Mr. Frampton would frequently go by on his horse with his sheep dog running alongside.

Swimming in the river. Mrs. Rawlings often took the children swimming in the river, which was used quite a lot while the beaches were wired off; then someone drowned at Cuckoo's Corner and it was stopped as too dangerous. [Cuckoo's Corner is on the west side of the river Adur, about half a mile north of Old Shoreham bridge.]

Country folk. I was educated at Evelyn House school in Buckingham Road, Shoreham, and then at The Towers at Beeding. My family left Steyning to farm in Kent. As my school friends tended to be country folk, my off duty time was spent with Mollie Strivens and her family at Old Erringham farm, and Mary & Peggy Passmore at Coombes, which is where I met their brother Dick. Shorty after we were married in 1946, he took over the running of the family farm where we now live. Diana Rawlings was my bridesmaid, and also godmother to our daughter Jennifer. The Rawlings boys were constant visitors, helping on the farm during their student years. I shall always remember those happy years with the Rawlings family.

65. 1930 view of Old Shoreham and St. Nicolas church from Lancing Ring, showing the fields and a lot of trees. The roof of the Sussex Pad is right of centre, with the old A27 and toll bridge beyond.

66. 1947 view looking S.E. over the Red Lion, before Old Shoreham Stores was built. Note the narrow lane in front of Perryman's shop and garden, now the access to the car park of the Amsterdam p.h.

THE ADUR VALLEY, SHOREHAM-BY-SEA. 3701.

67. 1920's view of the valley, waterworks road & toll bridge from Mill
Hill. The church & barns are top left. The white patch, left of centre, is
the chalk pit; now overgrown and just south of the A27 by-pass.

YE OLDE
RED LION
TAMPLIN'S ALES
WINES & SPIRITS
TEAS CAR PARK
OPPOSITE

68. Looking west across the railway from an attic window in 1946.
Wartime mooring posts can be seen in the river. J. Boxall, shoeing and
general smith, worked in the corrugated shed c. 1900.

69. Loading hay in the Adur valley c.1916. Percy Norman, farmer of Old Shoreham farm, is standing on the wagon with a pitch fork. Below, from the left, are H. W. Tingley, his son, Len Cobby, unknown.

70. The same event c.1916. The horse gin drives the elevator via a drive shaft. Percy Norman has his hands on his hips and H. W. Tingley is second left of him. The other men are mostly farm workers.

71. Old Shoreham school, October 1928, senior class (age 10-14)

Back row (5 boys standing on bench), left to right: Reg. Wm. Suter; Albert Tuppen; Anthony Priest; Alex Hancorn; Henry Johnson

Upper middle row (standing, 2 boys, 7 girls, 2 boys), left to right: Hubert Sinden; Briton Still; Violet Peters; Nellie Snook; Doris Saunders; Marjorie Knight; Ivy Fuller; Celia Snook; Doreen Virgo; Walter Hancorn; Ron Fuller.

Lower middle row (boy, 5 girls on bench, boy), left to right: Ernest Cooper; Elizabeth Grinstead; Violet Denton; Betty Tuppen; Constance Tompsett; Nellie Peters; Leonard Jordan.

Front row (7 boys sitting on ground), left to right: Henry Perham; Ray Tuppen; Fred Langrish; Stanley Bishop; Harry Wellstead; Percy Glew; Chris Bowyer.

72. Old Shoreham school, October 1928, junior class (age 7 to 10)

Back row (6 boys standing on bench) left to right: Ivor & Roy Gawn (twins); Robert Virgo; Edward Pretty; Albert Leslie Woolmington; Arthur Barker.

Upper middle row (12 boys standing) left to right. John Minter; John Cooper, Victor Saunders; Henry Baker; Bernard Cox; Harry Fuller; Malcolm Langrish; Richard Everest; Ernest Denton; Harold Glew; Robert Bowyer; Gerald Prince.

Lower middle row (7 girls sitting on bench plus boy kneeling) left to right: Jessica Saunders; Gladys Barker; Nellie Dorey; Ivy Jordan; Dorothy Perham; Marjery White; Irene Munnery; Victor Heather.

Front row (boy, 7 girls, boy,) left to right: Denis Hersey; Eileen Dye; Margaret Tompsett; Rowena Fuller; Winifred Tuppen; Doris Nellie Jordan; Elsie Snook; Jessie White; Reginald Woolmington.

73. Old Shoreham school, October 1928, infant class (age 5 to 8)

Back row (6 boys standing on bench) left to right: John Wells; Desmond Hunt; Wm. Richard Paris; Fredk. William Adams; James Sinden; Peter Saunders

Middle row (4 boys standing, 7 girls sitting on bench, 3 standing): Robert Minter; Cecil Johnstone; Donald Hamilton; Alfred Puttock; Dorothy Smith; Muriel Knight; Annie Fuller; Dorothy White; Doreen Woolmington; Evelyn Godley; Margaret Munnery; Heather Perham; Reginald Grinstead; Alfred Bowyer.

Front row (11 sitting on ground) left to right: George Sanders; Eileen Wells; Lily Gadd; Marjery Matthews; Albert Knight; Eileen Johnson; Mary Castle; Dorothy Wickham; John Sinden; Charles Dorey; Denis Still.

74L. Elm trees on Connaught Avenue c.1939 just before they were felled
to widen the road. The trees were up to 4 feet in diameter.
74R. Winifred Perryman ran Perryman's grocery shop until c.1960.

75. 1933 sketch, by J. Oakman, of Perryman's grocery shop. It was a
bakery for about 60 years prior to 1923. Part of the bakehouse is shown
on the right. Note the sign advertising 'garden teas'.

76. Lesser Foxholes in 1939, looking west towards the entrance porch. Nigel Rawlings, age four, is sitting in a dog basket by the west pond, which has the fountain operating. The house was built c.1932.

77. Looking east from a bedroom window of Lesser Foxholes, in 1938, across the newly planted $2^1/_2$ acre garden. Sister Wadey is sitting by the pond with baby Diana and Nigel. Adur Cottage is above centre.

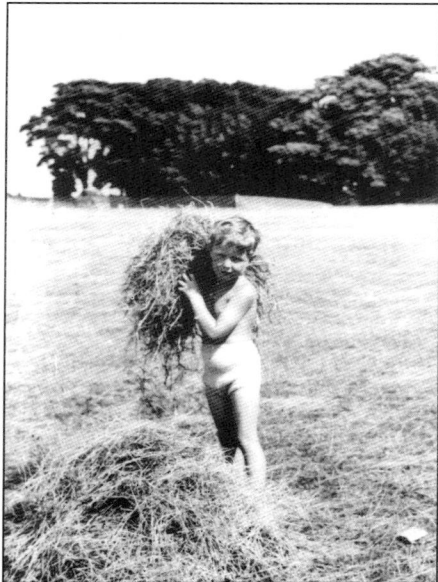

78L. Jack Rawlings with Christopher, Diana, Nigel & Richard in 1943.
78R. Nigel gathering hay in the paddock/field c.1942. Looking east, this photograph shows the elm trees along The Street.

79. The entrance to Lesser Foxholes, looking west from The Street c.1960. You could go in either side of the bank. Elm trees along the narrow lane contributed to its rural feel.

80. 1941 sketch of Adur Lodge by E. S. Stamp, looking north from the lawn. This view shows the building with two pitched roofs. The west roof was replaced by a flat roof soon after the army left in 1945.

81. Looking north up Mill Hill from The Street after the 1881 snow storm. Note the water company marker. On the east corner, right, was a pond known as Cockeroost pond. Cockeroost barn was further east.

82. An artist's view of Old Shoreham mill. The mill stood on the west side of Mill Hill, immediately north of the cutting for the modern A27 by-pass. It was built before 1780 and burned down c.1890.

83. The Mill House, Mill Hill c.1960. This is a view of the rear, looking north east. The living accommodation was on the ground floor and the upstairs was a miller's loft. Graeme Eager is on the roof.

84. Old Erringham manor house in 1967, looking N.W. It was split into farm cottages by 1850, but became a single dwelling again c.1970. The gate was the access to the cottages from Mill Hill.

85. Southdown Golf Club started at Buckingham barn in 1900. This new club house opened in 1903 at New Barn Lane. The land was taken over by the army in 1914. The club resumed at New Erringham in 1935.

86. Little Buckingham cottages in 1946, looking east towards the heavy horse stable. The road, now The Avenue, was then just a cart track passing through flint boundary walls. See map, illus. 46.

87. A similar view taken from a higher position in 1956, when development had started. The buildings, from the left, are the dovecote, machinery barn, cottages, cow stall, & heavy horse stable.

88. Looking east at Little Buckingham farm in 1958. The main cow stall is in the centre of the photo, the dovecote is on the left, and the granary is between them. To identify other buildings see illus. 45 & 46.

89. Buckingham House, looking N.W. c.1904. It was built c.1820, for the Bridger family, in classical style with doric columns. The girls are grand-daughters of Henry Head, who lived there from c.1890 to 1905.

90. Buckingham Lodge, the gate house to Buckingham House and park. It was situated north of the triangle of trees at the top of Buckingham Road. This photograph was taken in 1906 or earlier,

91. By 1911 the Lodge was rebuilt as shown here, probably while W. G. Little was the owner of Buckingham park. It was re-named Lodge Gate and is now No. 324 Upper Shoreham Road.

92L. William Virgo, page boy to the Head family at Buckingham House.
92R. Henry Head with his daughter Hester, and grand daughters, at Buckingham House c.1904.

93. Henry & Mrs. Head, centre, hosting a garden party on the lawn by Buckingham House c.1900. The Heads often entertained the local gentry, and held an annual produce & flower exhibition, with prizes.

94. The coachman for Buckingham House, looking rather fine in his tall hat; which suggests that the photograph was taken before the time of the motor car.

95. A new car in the drive at Buckingham park, in the early years of this century. The brick building was probably to the south west of the house, possibly south of the present Old Buckingham Mews.

96. The hunt meeting at Buckingham House c.1900. The hounds were kept in kennels at Buckingham park. The hunt went out to Drove Road [The Drive] via the 'hunting gate' on the west side of the park.

97. Trees lying across the drive to Buckingham House after the storm of 3 March 1897, when 82 trees fell in Buckingham park and the triangle. For a full contemporary account, see pages 120-1.

98. An event in Buckingham park c.1925 when the park was owned by E. R. Harrison. Events were usually declared open from the steps between the doric columns on the surviving east wall of the house.

99. The later Buckingham House, built by W. G. Little about 200 yards north of the old house. Mr. Harrison sold it c.1930. It was the Downs School in the 1930's, and a Children's Home after the war.

100. Upper Shoreham Road, looking east c. 1925. The triangle of trees is in the centre of the photo and Buckingham Road is off to the right. The man with his children is Mr. Walker from Southwick.

BUCKINGHAM LANE,
SHOREHAM BY-SEA.

101. Buckingham Road, looking north towards the triangle of trees c.1920. The footpaths were made for the soldiers during the 1914-18 war. The car, possibly a Renault, has registration number CD 951.

102. Looking north up Mill Lane, from Southdown Road, after the snow storm of January 1881. Overmead is now built left of centre. The kissing gate is off the photo, to the right.

103. 1914. The 'Kissing Gate', right, was at the south end of a path from Upper Shoreham Road to Mill Lane. The lower part survives. The wall, extreme right, belonged to Vicarage Lodge. See page 116.

104. Mill Lane, looking south c.1960, with Paul Plumb's May Day dancers. The cemetery lodge, right, is still there. Southdown Nurseries, centre, has gone. So has the elegant old gas street lamp.

105. The ex-servicemen's club, built after WW1, stood where Nos. 6 to 12 Connaught Avenue now stand. It was the Shoreham Grammar School gymnasium from c.1927. The Home Guard office was there during WW2.

106. Looking north from the tower of St. Mary's church in 1914. The rows of army tents, above and left of centre, are in the Oxen field, now Oxen Avenue. Note the number of trees beyond.

107. Shoreham camp in 1914. These rows of army tents are somewhere on the downs north of Shoreham, probably near Buckingham park. In 1915, rows of army huts were built to the north of Little Buckingham.

108. Another view of army tents in 1914, looking south towards Little Buckingham farm. The light spot to the right, by the trees, is Little Buckingham pond. The large building is the machinery barn.

109. Thomas Turrell (b.1849) and his wife Christiana (nee Reeve) at their home, No. 4 Hoopers Cottages, in 1931. The cottage is now the rear part of the Amsterdam p.h. Thomas was born at Old Erringham.

Lesser Foxholes

> Mr. Fred Tester (b. 1909) was the gardener at Lesser Foxholes and general helper to the family.

I was born in Portslade and I started work at the Lancing railway works but didn't like it. I spent two years in a blacksmiths shop, then went into market gardening, then building. I first went to Lesser Foxholes when I was working for Gates, the builders of Shoreham. We were doing repair works and alterations to the house.

Mr. & Mrs. Rawlings hadn't been married very long and had recently moved from London [late 1937]. They only had Nigel at that time. I spent some time there doing odd jobs, and Mrs. Rawlings asked if I would like to work for them as gardener. I carried on with Gates for a while but there was a shortage of work, so I took up Mrs. Rawlings offer. I worked there until I was called up, then went back to work for them after the war. I was always called 'Tess' by the family. During the war, George Bartlett looked after the garden.

Created ponds.   The Rawlings bought the [3½ acre] field to the north of the house and created a new large [2½ acre] garden in 1938. I helped to put the ponds in, then looked after the garden until I was called up. There was a pond at the top [east side of garden] and a waterfall down to the lower pond where the gold-fish were.

Animals.   The remaining northern part of the field [2 acres] was grazing for the children's ponies. They had all sorts of animals for the children's interest; geese, chickens, guinea fowl, rabbits. At one stage they borrowed some sheep from Old Shoreham farm so that the children could see the lambs. They had about 50 chickens so we got lots of eggs.

I was treated like one of the family and still am. I was invited to all the weddings and parties. Mrs. Rawlings was a lady; very well brought up. They were both very nice people.

Business in London & Shoreham.   Mr. Rawlings had an electrical business in London and went there by train. He also owned the Sussex Shipbuilding Co. on Shoreham Beach, which made naval craft and torpedo boats during the war. Mr. Rawlings had his own yacht and was Rear Commodore of the Sussex Yacht Club in 1950.

Learned to drive.   Mr. Rawlings had an Armstrong Siddeley car which he drove to the station. I drove it back for two weeks in second gear because I didn't know how to change gear. I borrowed the car one Sunday and a friend showed me how to do it. After that I drove the car on errands and acted as taxi driver to the family in addition to looking after the garden, the horses and the other animals. You did not need to take a driving test in those days, and you didn't need a driving licence.

Slept in the car.   After the war, I frequently drove Mr. Rawlings to Bath on Fridays to discuss naval contracts. I drove him there during Thursday night, and brought him back the following night. He slept in the car on the way. I once stopped for breakfast at a farm house while he was asleep in the car. I didn't tell him. I slept whilst he was at the meeting, ready to drive him back. Mr. Rawlings had a number of different cars, he changed his car every two years. I remember a Daimler, a Morris, a Singer and a Bentley.

Supervised the children. The nanny was in charge of the children when they were inside the house and I was in charge when they were outside. I was allowed to punish them if they were naughty, perhaps give them a job to do or stop them playing, but I was always fair. They had known me from childhood and respected me. I drove the children to school and, later, drove them to the station to go to work. I was there by 6.30 in the morning. They got a taxi back, or walked.

Tyrant cook. They had a number of cooks over the years, but I don't remember any names. Most of them were good. There was one who was a bit of a tyrant and wouldn't let anyone into the kitchen. Even Mrs. Rawlings wasn't allowed in there after 10 a.m. I told the cook that I had always been allowed in the kitchen to make myself a cup of coffee, and if she stopped me she would have to get the vegetables and pluck the birds. I was then allowed in. She was getting on and didn't last long.

Gladys Stoner was the parlour maid. She lived on The Street, round the corner from Adur Lodge [Durhamside].

Tennis courts. There was a kitchen garden, and fruit bushes, such as blackberry, which were under wire netting to stop the birds eating the fruit. There were yew hedges with openings through, and herbaceous borders. They had two tennis courts; one grass and one with a hard surface. The boys from Lancing College often came to use them because they were all tennis mad.

Siamese cats for Harrods. They had gold-fish in the pond. The eggs were transferred to a separate maternity pond so they wouldn't be eaten by the fish. The fish were sold each year to Harrods in London. We also bred and sold siamese cats to Harrods, and budgerigars. I got a share of the proceeds. The aviary was by the south side of the house.

Sold for development. When Lesser Foxholes was sold [c.1966] I started my own business as a landscape gardener. My first job was the landscaping of all the gardens on the new Lesser Foxholes development for Fenix Ltd. of London. I had to repair all the damage done by lorries around the house [now known as Foxholes Lodge]. I was doing that for about a year, making up the ground as people moved in. Many of them employed me to look after their gardens afterwards. I put in the swimming pool for the new owners of the house [Foxholes Lodge].

Mrs. Ivy Priest (b.1910), sister of Fred Tester, has lived on The Street since 1938 and worked at Lesser Foxholes.

Ropetackle. I came to Shoreham from Portslade in 1932 when I married Wallace Bradford, who was known as Joe. We lived at No. 5 Little High Street with his father, Charles Bradford, who was a fisherman. Little High Street was at Ropetackle, between the Kings Head p.h. and Slaughters greengrocery shop. I had never even cooked a potato before, but I had to start cooking for my husband, his brother and his father. We had to leave there in 1938 because they wanted to demolish the cottages.

Joe was a brick layer, plasterer and tiler. He was working for Percy Payne, the builder, on these six houses [south of No. 5 The Street]. We moved here when this house was completed in 1938. Just before the war, Joe worked for Mr. Rawlings at the Sussex Shipbuilding Co. He helped to launch the boats when they were testing them. During the war, Joe was sent to Lakenheath airfield in Suffolk, along with other builders. He was allowed home one weekend every two months.

Laundry. The Rawlings were short of staff during the war because of call-ups. Nanny Chandler asked me if I knew anyone who could help out. As Joe was away, I started to work part time at Lesser Foxholes, washing clothes & ironing. There were no washing machines then, we had to kneel down by the bath to do it. Nanny Chandler and I also shared the house work. Later, they bought a washing machine.

Cooking. When their cook left, I began doing the cooking, but not for the evening meal. I made jams, jellies, christmas cakes, anything! I never had any training; I picked it up as I went along. Richard Rawlings (b.1941) was just crawling when I first went there. I worked there for three hours every morning, six days a week, until they sold the house in the 1960's. I sometimes went over there on Sunday morning to put the lunch in the oven.

Holiday. A girl called 'Tweeny', who was about 14 years old, was working there after the war. We all went to the Isle of Wight for a months holiday in a bungalow. Mrs. Rawlings hired a coach and we went with their friends named Mason, who lived on Lancing sea front. I did all the catering and Tweeny helped me. I remember that there was still rationing at the time.

Our house was like a second home for the Rawlings children, who always came in through our back door and would introduce me to their friends. I sometimes baby sat, and Peter came here to sleep if they had visitors and were short of space.

Mr. Rawlings was on the rota for the Home Guard, answering the telephone. The Home Guard office was in the gymnasium on the Shoreham Grammar School playing field [see photo 105]. It was built just after the 1914-18 war as a club for ex-servicemen. Mr. Rawlings often took surplus vegetables to give away.

Mrs. Zoe Ellman-Brown (b.1904) and her husband, John Ellman-Brown, bought Adur Lodge, former home of the Bridger family, in 1943 when it was occupied by the army.

When I was about 12 years old [c.1916] we came down from Lancashire to Shoreham Beach for a holiday. My mother and step-father decided to move down permanently. The bungalow in which we stayed was called 'Simplicity' and was owned by Ernie Mayne, a famous stage artiste of the day. I subsequently met my late husband, John Ellman-Brown and we were married in 1932. He was an estate agent and the grandson of the original John Ellman Brown [1826-1910], who was a ship broker & Lloyds agent. It was he who started the family estate agency in 1896. The name 'Ellman' came from his mother Jane Ellman, whose great uncle Thomas Ellman farmed Buckingham farm. [He ran the farm from 1780 to 1806 and was recognised as an innovative farmer. His cousin John Ellman of Glynde was presented with a cup in 1805 for his services to agriculture.]

After our marriage, we lived on Shoreham Beach in a bungalow called 'Wendy' for a few years, then moved to a house called 'Four Views' on the south-west side of Mill Hill, which may previously have been called 'White Cottage'. The well-known comedian Fred Emney lived there in the 1950's.

Adur Lodge [see illus. 80]

In 1943, we bought Adur Lodge, The Street, from Mr. Frank Bridger. It was then occupied by the army. After the war, whilst it was being repaired and modernised following the ravages of army occupation, we rented a bungalow named 'Wellesley' on Shoreham Beach. We finally moved into Adur Lodge in 1946, I believe. [The Bridger family lived at Adur Lodge from about 1890, after they left Buckingham House.]

The house and gardens were on almost two acres. There were grape vines [still there] in the conservatory on the south side of the house and roses growing up the wrought-iron supports for the veranda. We had a billiard room in the south-west of the house. The old coach house was at the north-east corner of the land [No. 1 Lodge Court now stands there]. We kept the gardening equipment in the coach house and put the ducks in there at night. We also kept a dozen geese on the large area of land to the south and we grew all our own vegetables in the kitchen garden. There was a well in the garden to the south of the conservatory [east of the existing well, which is set into the tall west wall and currently covered by a large flower pot].

In July 1950 we sold the whole property to a Mr. Matthews who had been showing an interest in the purchase for some time. He, in turn, sold about two thirds of the land to Mr. E. G. Parker and the present Lodge Court development was erected later on this land. We moved to Dolphin House on Buckingham Road, near the triangle of trees, and subsequently back to Shoreham Beach - thus completing the circle!

Mrs. Heather Clark (nee Eager) was born at the Mill House in 1935. The remains of the old mill were in their garden. Her grandfather was Station Master at Shoreham railway station.

The Eagers are an old Sussex family from the Glynde area. Grandfather, Joseph Henry Eager, was a station master at various railway stations. He moved to Station Villa, Brunswick Road, Shoreham about 1905 and died there in 1923.

My father, Charles Allan Eager, known as Allan, left the Merchant Navy due to ill health in 1919, then worked on a farm in Findon. In the General Strike of 1926 he drove milk lorries in London to various hospitals. After moving back to Sussex with my mother he did various work, including farm management, milk roundsman, and boat building. My mother, Hovie, was born in South Shields and married my father there in 1925. My eldest brother Bruce was born at Streatham in 1926. Iain was born at Burgess Hill in 1928, and Graeme at Old Shoreham Road in 1931. I was born at the Mill House in 1935.

The Mill House was then the last house at the top of Mill Hill on the west side [see photo 83]. It stood on a rectangular plot of land of about $^3/_4$ acre. The house stood centrally on the east side of our land, close to the road. The paddock, about $^1/_4$ acre, was on the west side of the plot, with the vegetable garden between that and the house. Our driveway was along the south edge of our land, with a gate at the road, and another into the paddock. Between the driveway and the house was an orchard (nearest the road) and the lawn.

The remains of the old mill were on our land, to the north of the vegetable garden. You can still see a small section of the mill wall on the north bank of the A27 by-pass [in the hedge on the north side of the public footpath]. [An artist's sketch of the mill is shown in illus. 82.]

Millers loft. The living accommodation was all at ground floor level. The roof area was formerly the millers loft, where the sacks of corn were stored. The loft was reached via thick timber steps on the outside of the house, north side. In our time this was fathers 'Den'.

To enter the house, the front door was straight off the road, through a small porch and so into the living room. Beyond [west of] the living room was the dining room, which later became my bedroom. To the north of the living room and dining room were two bedrooms. Oh how cold those bedrooms could be in the winter.

We didn't use the front door very much. We came indoors through the back (kitchen) door via the big gate and the driveway past the orchard, then across the lawn to the kitchen. The kitchen was in the south west corner of the house and the bathroom in the south east corner. These rooms had brick flooring whereas the rest of the house had floor boards. The kitchen was always warm with the kitchener burning all the time for cooking and, from 1939, to heat the water as well.

The walls were very thick, so it was a good solid building, especially when the south west wind blew.

The garden soil was very shallow when my parents first moved to the Mill House in the early 1930's. It was just a few inches in depth over chalk. Father dug and collected earth from the centre ground of the mill and so gradually built up the soil level for our vegetable garden. There were some fruit trees. To make cream cheese, we hung curdled milk, in a tied-up white cloth, on the plum tree. The west part of our land was a paddock where the goats grazed and the chickens roamed.

We had lots of animals over the years. There were out-buildings where the chickens and our 2 or 3 goats were put at night. At one time we had a poorly lamb which Mr. Frampton gave to father. He kept it alive for a few weeks but sadly it died in the end. During the war we looked after at least one pig for Mr. Batten.

Blackberrying. When I was young, mother often took we four children over the downs blackberrying for most of the day. We picked loads and brought them home to be cooked with apples, and subsequently made into jam and pies. I sometimes went out very early, with my brothers, to pick mushrooms from the field on the other side of the road, east of the reservoir.

Covered the chimney pots. In the summer, the June bugs would fly in hundreds, particularly in the early evening. Father would climb up onto the roof and tie sacking over the chimney pots (except the kitchen) to keep them out. They didn't sting you at all, but were a nuisance.

Wartime. During the last war there were Nissen huts and soldiers and a gun on the triangular piece of land adjoining ours on the north side. There were also soldiers and guns further down Mill Hill. [There was a first world war boxing arena cut into the chalk approx. 150 yards east of Mill House, i.e. on the east side of Mill Hill.]

Mr. & Mrs. Bobby lived next door to us. They shared our underground air raid shelter during the war. This was at the end of our driveway. I was told that this was a deep cess pit when we first moved there. When the war came, father and others constructed some steps, put a strong top on it, and covered it with turf. Mr. & Mrs. Avis lived at the next house down, Red Gables. My father was a Special Constable with Mr. Avis during the war.

[Mr. & Mrs. Bobby lived at 'The Downs', built between the Mill House and Red Gables in the late 1930's. These three houses disappeared with the cutting for the A27 Shoreham by-pass, along with the old boxing arena.]

It was a hard working life for our parents, but we were all happy and I have fond memories.

My husband Alfred was born in 1902. He worked at Ricardo's for most of his life as an engineer. We moved here in December 1936, after we married. Ours was the first house to be built along here, east of Adur Lodge.

Poultry farm. This site, south of Mill Hill, was a poultry farm which had belonged to Squire Bridger of Adur Lodge. Jack Parlett, the builder, had bought it for development when we first came to look at it in 1935. The gate to the poultry farm was at the front of our house. Mr. Parlett built the other houses as he got orders. He built Galleons Reach for Mr. Gunning, who kept chickens on the land at the bottom of our garden.

Cows on the garden. Mr. Parlett did not put up proper fences, so we frequently found cows and sheep on our front garden, but we didn't mind. The field opposite, now the grazing field, was regularly used for lambing. Mr. Tuppen had his shepherd's hut in the corner, near the gate, at lambing time. Another year they would grow corn in the field again, and Mr. Tuppen's hut would then be at Mossy Bottom or wherever they were lambing. Before the war, they used an elevator to get hay and corn up into the wagon [see photo 70].

Gas street lamp. An old chap came up every day on his bike when it was time to light the gas street lamp. The lamp outside our gate was already here when we moved in. It was all grass out there. The Avenue was nothing then, just lovely fields. The cows came up twice a day from Old Shoreham farm to graze in the fields north of Hazelcroft. There were no houses along there. Capt. Torr's land was further along [east]. When the children went to school they often had to dodge the cows from Old Shoreham farm.

Cockeroost pond. We sometimes saw badgers crossing the lane. At the bottom of Mill Hill, on the east corner, there was a pond [see photo 81]. Alfred called it Cockeroost pond. It collected water that came down the hill, but it was stagnant and a bit smelly.

The tramps came past here on their way from the workhouse at East Preston to the Steyning Union workhouse, which is now Southlands Hospital. An old boy with a long beard and a billy can would knock on the door in the early evening and ask for water to make tea. You knew when they were there because you would see their smoke going up near the pond. They went on to the workhouse later. If they got there too early they were given a job to do.

Subsidence. About 1960, the pond was suddenly filled with earth, then an architect named Hunt built a house over the pond. It was unusual because it faced east. After it had changed hands a couple of times it started to subside. It was underpinned with concrete. After a while it started to subside again and it had to be pulled down. The owner built two new houses on the site.

Mr. Brian Bazen (b.1928) worked at Southlands Hospital during the war. His father drove a steam lorry for the Beeding cement works.

Father drove steam lorry.   My father, William Bazen, worked for the Beeding cement works and drove a Foden steam lorry c.1930. He frequently drove it along Steyning Road & Old Shoreham Road. During the war he was in the Home Guard. One night, several bombs dropped on the cement works. One of them damaged the railway line as a goods train was approaching. He managed to stop the train by waving a lamp and later received a letter of thanks from Southern Railway. I was born in Surry Street in 1928. In 1943 I started work as a patient record clerk at Southlands Hospital. I learned German at night classes at Middle Road school. I joined the army (R.A.M.C.) in 1946.

Bombs.   I was walking over Old Shoreham bridge with my cousin when the sirens first sounded after war was declared on Sunday 3 September 1939. I was then 11 years old. The first bomb fell just to the south of Buckingham barn and made a hole in the field, where the A27 Shoreham by-pass is now built. The bombs which dropped on Buckingham Street were aimed at the railway viaduct. I saw the three bombs leave the aeroplane. German bombers frequently used the river Adur as a navigation aid and flew over Lancing College.

Germans shot down.   I remember seeing a Germam Messerschmitt 109 being chased by a Hurricane. It was shot down and crash landed on the downs between Mill Hill and Buckingham barn. I collected small parts from crashed aeroplanes and bombs as souvenirs and kept them in a biscuit tin. Whilst I was working at Southlands Hospital, a German airman was shot down over Shoreham and brought in. I knew a little German from my night classes and was asked to try to get his personal information. He would only give his name and number.

I took photos of the grave of another German airman shot down over Shoreham, a Flug. Lieutnant Pulwer. He was buried at Shoreham cemetery on Mill Lane. I sent photographs to his relatives in Germany after the war, at Bad Salzuflen, and they wrote to thank me. I believe his remains were later taken to Germany.

Nudged a doodlebug.   During the latter part of the war c.1944 I actually saw a spitfire nudge a flying bomb, coming over Shoreham, and turn it back in the direction of the English Channel.

Adur Lodge was occupied by the army during the war. I remember seeing Italian prisoners-of-war doing manual work there. They wore clothing supplied by the War Office, with a distinctive arrow motif. Patches were sewn to their knees, to be shot at if they tried to escape. They were never a menace and some of them had good singing voices.

Len Tuppen (b.1912) lived on Steyning Road and worked at Little Buckingham farm. He drove the horse and cart. His father was the shepherd from 1928.

Stuck in the country.   When father first came to Shoreham to see about working at Little Buckingham farm, Capt. Torr took him to the cottage where we would live. It was beyond the golf course and rabbit warren, surrounded by a hedge. Before they got there, Capt. Torr pointed out where it was. Father said we could not live there because mother had been stuck out on the downs all her life and now wanted to be near the shops and a Post Office. Capt. Torr took him to Old Shoreham village and showed him the cottage on Steyning Road. There was someone living there [the Sindens] but Capt. Torr said they could be out within a week [see photos 5 & 6].

Carried out.   The day we arrived in Old Shoreham in 1928 we got there about 9 a.m. They [the Sindens] hadn't packed anything and were eating their breakfast. Father wanted to get on with it. We hung about outside for a while, then father told us that as soon as they finished their breakfast we were to start carrying everything out. As soon as they got up from the table we carried it out onto the grass. They didn't get time to wash up. They didn't have a lot of furniture anyway. When father said to do something you had to do it, whatever it was! [The Sindens left Shoreham in Oct. 1928.]

Thatching.   One of the first jobs I had at Shoreham was thatching a cottage with Mr. Fuller [senior] near the Beeding cement works. As you leave Dacre Gardens there was a cottage on the bend, on the west side of the road by a barn. The road was then right in front of the houses at Dacre Gardens but has since been moved. George Bailey, a shepherd, lived there. George Fuller went there to thatch the roof. I went there with him to draw the straw. You had to wet the straw first, then pull it into a strod. You never worked with dry straw. The strod was an open channel, about 3 feet long, about 15 inches wide at one end and narrowing down to a few inches at the other end. You would put the strod on the ground and lay the wet straw in it, with a heavy piece of wood on top to hold it down tight. When the strod was full you carried it up to the thatcher.

Kept outside.   The thatching ladders were long and had to lay on the slope of the roof. The foot of the ladder stood well out into the road, which was very close. You could not do that today with all the traffic. It took us a week or two to do the job, but Mrs. Bailey would not let us go indoors. If it rained we had to shelter in the chicken house.

Steyning market.   When I was driving the milk float for Little Buckingham farm [see account on p.56], I did other jobs between the morning and evening milk runs. If it was Monday I had to load up with whatever was going to Steyning market. It might be chickens, sheep, calves or a pig. I went past home, along Steyning Road. After unloading at Steyning I went home for my dinner. I left the horse on the piece of grass south of our cottage.

Winter sprouts. After dinner I might have to see Harry Holmes to collect whatever had to go to Brighton. A lot of sprouts and cabbages were grown on the farm for sale in winter. I took it to Black Lion Street in Brighton. By the time I came back along the sea front it was dark and cold. The cabbage business died out just before I left the farm [1931].

Young cattle. When I got back from Brighton I did the evening milk run. That was when I was driving the float, almost a full time job. At other times I was looking after the young cattle stock which were all up over the hills. There were a lot at Hill barn [Buckingham barn]. From there I walked to Happy Valley barn, where there were more cattle. From there I went to Mossy Bottom, where there were more cattle, then I came back to Little Buckingham farm.

Harry Holmes is the man in photo 60. His job on the farm was to grow the vegetables: sprouts, cabbages, peas etc. He was a clever chap. He could do all sorts of odd jobs that many of us could not. He grew the vegetables on about 5 acres of land along the south side of Upper Shoreham Road, between Buckingham Road and Eastern Avenue. There were a few allotments along there as well, at the eastern end, and more down the back [south].

Molasses. When we had lunch in the barn where the cow food was stored, Harry Holmes sat on a barrel of molasses, a sort of black treacle that was mixed in with the cow food. Harry would take the bung out, dip a stick in there and have some with his bread and cheese. 'Good for the blood' he would say. I don't know where Harry lived, probably the town.

Mr. Spiers was foreman at the farm when I went there. He was not a Sussex man. I believe he was from the west country. [He died suddenly, about 1932.]

Nick Mayler was a carter at the farm. He looked after the horses and lodged in a house behind the Amsterdam [at No. 3 Hoopers Cottages in 1929]. He left shortly after I started there. Stan Fuller took over his job.

Jim Scott was the head cowman at the farm. He lived a few doors south of the Fullers [at No.19]. He gave us all nick names. He left when I was at the farm, and I never saw him again until about 1970, when I met him at Newick, Sussex, where we were both doing a flower show. I had no idea he was living so close to me.

Cricket. Jim Scott was very fond of cricket. There was a field at the back of the Fullers home, Walnut Cottage, where we played cricket of an evening.

Bill Short was a labourer on the farm and lived somewhere in Shoreham town. Fred Luther was a cowman come labourer. There is a picture of him in your book [photo 57]. He lived in a cottage which is now part of the Amsterdam p.h. [No. 21 Old Shoreham.]

Farr, Kelly & Wiffin. Will Farr was a cowman. He was getting on. He lived on The Street, in the thatched cottage later occupied by Joe Kelly [No. 8]. Joe Kelly rode the race horses for Capt. Torr. I knew Joe Kelly before he came to Shoreham. He worked at George Pool's racing stables in Lewes. Charlie Wiffin lived in a bungalow near the farm.

Rats. My brother Albert looked after the chickens. The runs were alive with rats but they never did anything to get rid of them. When he gave it up my brother Raymond took it over full time, but not for long. When the war came he pretended he was older, to join the army. He never came back from the war.

Maize field. As you went up the road to the farm [now Downsway], the land to the west, as far as Erringham Road, was used for growing vegetables as well as crops [see photo 60]. I believe they had just started building on the east side of Erringham Road when I left the farm.

Cockeroost. The Nye's lived at Hazelcroft, near Cockeroost. Cockeroost barn was an old building. A few cows were kept there at one time. I walked through there to get to the farm, or cycled along the main road.

The triangle. I sometimes met up with an old shepherd named Trigwell. I never knew where he lived, but he often sat on the public seat at the south point of the triangle of trees, looking down Buckingham Road. He was retired then. He sat there with another old boy. I never knew which farm he had worked on. He was a cheeky old boy, quite a character. I liked talking to the old ones. There were several shepherds from the Trigwell family.

Cultivated land. In my time there was no cultivated land until you left the farm and got up past the 'camp ground', through the valley towards Erringham Farm. There were about 4 or 5 acres there, where they grew wheat, and on top of the brow they had another 2 acres, then no more until you got to Mossy Bottom valley. When I first went there they were growing potatoes at Mossy Bottom, and again the following year. There was no more arable ground until you got to Crooked Moon, where there were probably another 6 or 7 acres. That was all the arable land that Little Buckingham farm had on the downs.

Hay making. We did quite a lot of hay making between Mossy Bottom & Crooked Moon, but there was never enough for the number of cattle and sheep they had. They never had enough straw to bed the cattle down. We would go down to White's timber yard and spend all day long bagging up chippings. It was used in the cow stalls for bedding, and it blocked up the drains something shocking. All the slurry went down the drains. We were forever unblocking them.

Pasture at Golding Barn. Capt. Torr had some brooks [pasture lands] near Golding Barn, between Beeding and Small Dole. We drove the cattle up Mill Hill, past Erringham farm and the rabbit warren, over Beeding Hill and down towards Golding Barn. I remember us cutting hay over there. I had to take the men in the cart. George & Stan Fuller would put their bicycles in the cart so they could cycle home. We had to put the hay in trusses, load the wagon and stack it. It was brought back to the farm as it was needed, not all at once. Two wagon loads might last a week or so.

Summersdene farm. Capt. Torr also had Summersdene farm, at a place called Rats Ramble about a mile north of Mile Oak water works, towards Truleigh Hill. If you went up through the farm to the brow, you could look down onto the Shepherd & Dog p.h. at Fulking. We had to go there hay making, and again I had to take the men in the cart. I brought the men back as well. When we got near to Shoreham, George & Stan Fuller would cycle the rest of the way. They would put their bicycles on the cart again the next morning if we were going back there. I left home at 5.30 a.m. and spent all day at Summersdene. It might be 9.30 p.m. before I got back. I then had to feed the horses with oats, chaff or hay, and groom them while they were eating, before turning them out for the night. You had to give them time to have their food before turning them out. It was 10.30 or 10.45 p.m. before I got home. When Capt. Torr left Summersdene farm it had to be put back to how it was when he took it over. I remember that steam engines were used to plough it.

Hardly saw father. My father [the shepherd] and I were sleeping in the same cottage and working on the same farm but we didn't see each other all week. I saw him in the fields when I was going around the farm, but I didn't see him to talk to. He had gone to bed by the time I got home and I left before him in the morning.

Carters lot. They had six cart horses at Little Buckingham farm. They were never left indoors overnight, winter or summer. They were always put out, either on the camp ground [north of the farm buildings] or further along towards the back of Buckingham park. I took a turn every third week with George & Stan Fuller to go and get the horses in. The horses had to be in the stable by 6 a.m. When it was my turn I had to leave home at 5.30 a.m. The horses were not always where you left them. I remember once when I had to go over to Southwick for them because someone had left the gate open.

Pushed the pram. My [future] wife, Alice, worked for the Framptons in Old Shoreham farmhouse as a domestic servant. She was there when Hazel was born in 1932. When Alice came out with the pram on a Sunday I used to go with her and push the pram round all over the place. Alice's father, Albert Newman, and her brothers Bill & Ron were cow men at Old Shoreham farm, but were not there long.

Southdown Golf Club. My brothers and I went to work at the golf course at one time, cutting turfs, but we only stayed there about 3 weeks because we could not get on with the foreman. [The Southdown Golf Club started in 1900. It operated from Buckingham barn until 1903, when a new club house opened at what is now the south end of New Barn Lane - see photo 85. The golf course was requisitioned by the army in 1914. Attempts were made from c. 1927 to re-open the course and a new golf course opened in 1935. The club house was an old building at New Erringham, probably the former home of farmer Richard Sharpe 1847-66. This later club house caught fire during the 1939-45 war and was then used for target practice.]

112

Little Buckingham

> Mrs. Penelope Biggs (b.1916) is the eldest daughter of Capt. John Harold Torre Torr and his first wife Freda. She was at Little Buckingham from c.1920.

Capt. Torr & Freda. My father, known as Harold, married my mother, Freda Lindsell, in 1912. They moved from Oxford to Molash, Kent, where father attended Wye Agricultural College. Their income was a settlement of £300 a year each. On this they kept horses and a groom, hunted, and had a cook and a parlour maid. Father joined up in 1914 with the Lincolnshire Yeomanry. He left the army after the war with the rank of Captain.

Mother was skilled at embroidery and needle work as well as music and languages. She spoke French & German fluently, and had travelled widely in Europe, with her mother. She learned to play the violin at Dresden. She met father through his youngest sister, Dona, who was also studying the violin at Dresden. She invited my mother home to Cheshire.

Army huts from the 1914-18 war still covered the downs at the back of the house when we arrived at Little Buckingham c.1920. Most of them were soon demolished, leaving a kind of archaeological site of foundations which were fun to play on and around. A few of the huts were retained as hen houses.

Mother died. Rosalys, my sister, was born at Little Buckingham in November 1921. Mother died the following year, on 22 September, aged 36. I can remember mother out in the garden, organising the layout with the gardener, who we knew as 'Old Ashie'. Mother played the piano. One of my earliest memories of life at Little Buckingham is of learning my first scales with her at the Steinway piano, which I later inherited.

Little Buckingham house. The piano was in the 'music room' at Little Buckingham, where we also had a gramophone with a 'trumpet' speaker. The music room was in the south west corner of the house, at the front of the taller and more modern wing [see photo 49]. Father's library was in the music room, and behind was father's office. The rest of the house was lower and older, and the floors were on different levels.

The nursery wing was above the music room and father's office, on the west side of the house. My bedroom was at the back, over father's office. It had the most beautiful wallpaper, specially chosen by my mother, a deep powder blue with sprays of wonderfully realistic cherry blossom scattered over it. It was lovely to wake up to it in the early morning light. The day nursery, with a bay window, was at the front, over the music room. Between them was Nanny's room. There were back stairs from my bedroom to a large landing. Across this landing, on the east side of the house and above the kitchen, was the bathroom.

A four poster bed is the most memorable feature of mother's room, which was at the front of the house, adjacent to the day nursery, but with stairs down into it. I went in there in the mornings and sometimes watched mother brush her hair, which fell below her knees. Rosalys now has the bed.

The bathroom & dressing room were above the kitchen quarters [N.E. corner of the house], on the first floor. The bathroom was enormous. I can remember father shaving with his cut-throat razor, after 'stropping' it on the leather strop hung beside the basin, whilst I had my morning bath. I was fascinated to see his face covered in lather. In the bathroom, near the door, hung a row of copper cans, from small to very large, for taking water to the bedrooms and nursery. In those rooms there were no basins with running water, but wash stands with marble tops, china basins and ewers.

Lessons at Buckingham House. I remember, early on, being sent to share lessons and a governess with the Harrison girl who lived in [the later] Buckingham House [see photo 99]. After this I went to Miss Lea in New Shoreham. I was walked to New Shoreham by Alice, the nursery-maid, who lived-in.

Donkey and goat. We had a donkey, Ned, who would sit down in the field and beg like a dog, pawing with one hoof, for carrots or apples. He would also sit down in the shafts of the donkey cart in which we would go for picnics. He often refused to get up again, which was not so amusing. We had a goat who would consume anything except tins and bottles, and was often tethered for this purpose beside the back door or in front of the kitchen window.

Crops and hay making. I remember the field on the west side of 'our drive' - the muddy lane leading up to the house and farm from the main road [now called Downsway] - being used sometimes for hay, sometimes for wheat and sometimes for maize for cattle fodder. At hay making times we all turned out to help in the old way with long rakes, gathering the hay first into lines, then into hay-cocks to dry out. When it was thoroughly dry the hay-cocks would be pitchforked up to the waiting wagon, and the men would balance the load. When fully loaded the wagon was driven to the site chosen for the hay stack, which had to be carefully built and finally thatched. When the crop was wheat, I remember a steam thresher being used.

War was declared [3 September 1939] while I was working in London. During the summer of 1940, farming became impossible because of the tanks, and the Battle of Britain raging overhead [August 1940]. I recall a telegram from my father which read 'Come home. Have been living on Kit Kat for 3 days'. [Kit Kat then had a blue wrapper.] I got home to find father had sent my stepmother and the children to Devon [the lease was due to expire on 11 October 1940.] The rest of our time at Little Buckingham was eventful and unorthodox. The sale or transport of farm stock, machinery and implements had to be organised. Only one of the riding horses went with us to Devon. It was a busy time with a certain amount of entertaining to be done. I remember, having baked a large pie for expected guests, I crawled along the foot of the vegetable garden wall, with a cabbage to go with it, whilst a battle raged overhead.

Little Buckingham

Mrs. Rosalys Coope (b. 1921), the younger daughter of Capt. John Harold Torre Torr and his first wife Freda, was born at Little Buckingham.

The paddock in front of our house was large and had several very fine trees. Cattle were grazed there. I remember at least two annual fairs held there. On one occasion my step-mother opened it. It was a great thrill to have the merry-go-round and other amusements in front of the house. When the paddock was built over I was very saddened.

'Ashie' the gardener was a very kind man with a beard. He made me a little garden of my own, with two special seats made from the trunks of trees. This was in the garden, near the walled vegetable garden where I mostly remember him working. When Iris was born (1926), or possibly John (1928), I went to stay with him and his wife in the town. I remember seeing the gas-lighter going along the street lighting the gas street lamps.

Lessons at Greystones. Before I went to school, I had lessons at Greystones with Roger James and a couple of other children. I was taken down The Street to a place where there was a stile, or a gate, into a piece of land owned by Mr. James. I would run from there to the house; watched until I got there. We were taught in a large sitting room with a bay window by Miss Lea, one of two sisters who lived in Ravens Road. I remember The Street was very picturesque with a number of thatched cottages. Kelly, our jockey/groom lived in one of them.

Wiffin, the head groom, lived in a rather flimsy bungalow which lay to the east of our garden. One day, with great daring, Iris and I decided to go into Shoreham town, which we were strictly forbidden to do on our own, to visit Woolworths. Wiffin saw us and we got into trouble. Kelly and Wiffin were usually in the tack room at the end of the racehorse stable. Kelly was our friend and often entertained us. Over the stable was a loft for the hay and we were allowed to play up there.

Fir Cone Wood was our name for a small wood between our tennis court and Wiffin's garden. I played there frequently with Iris and John. To the south of the wood was a rather wide track of grass, running east out of the gravel sweep in front of Little Buckingham house to The Drive. I now think that was once part of the original upper road from the ferry, which ran along the line of The Avenue.

More trees. There was another small wood at the corner of our drive and what is now The Avenue, south of the heavy horse stable [see map, illus. 46]. We were there one day when an R101 airship came over. Father kept pointing to this wonderful thing, but I could not see it. We discovered that I was very short-sighted. A great ilex tree stood on the other side from the racehorse stable, and a bit further south. It was a beautiful tree. There were some magnificent elm trees beyond the farm gate to the north, near the ricks and pond. Father was particularly fond of those [see photos 51 & 53].

The farm was a wonderful place for children to grow up. We played there and watched the work going on. The cow shed seemed enormous and the number of cows formidable. All the milking was done by hand. Of the cow men, I remember Ernie Sayers best. The sterilizing plant at the end of the cow shed was, I recollect, ruled over by Mr. Bishop. We were very fond of looking at the calves in the calf pens.

Mr. Spiers [the farm bailiff] was rather an alarming figure to me. He had a very high colour and a bristly dark moustache. His wife was gentle and faded-looking. One summers day, when we were sitting in the garden having tea, Mrs. Spiers came rushing up in a terrible state to tell us that Mr. Spiers had had a great fit and fallen down dead. I was probably age eleven at the time [c.1932]. It all seemed very dramatic to us children. George Fuller then became father's right hand man. He was a great friend to us children. His brother Stan was in charge of the heavy horses and was marvellous with them. Mr. Tuppen, the shepherd, was also a great friend. He taught me a lot about the weather and what to look for to tell how it would be.

The granary was a curious black building on stilts, near the dovecote. It had big bins divided by wooden partitions and we were fond of going in there and burying ourselves in the grain. It was great fun, but was not encouraged by the grown-ups.

The milk float. When I was older, I liked to drive the milk float down to the dairy in Shoreham with the churns from the afternoon milking. Jumbo, who pulled it, was a rather lazy cob; one had to keep him going! It is amazing to think how little traffic there was. In our day we called the town New Shoreham and 'our' Shoreham was Old Shoreham.

Rural and quiet roads. Before I went off to boarding school, c.1926, I often went for walks with the nanny or governess. We frequently walked to the workhouse, now Southlands Hospital, and this name conjured up some Dickensian visions in our minds when we were young. Another favourite walk was to and over the wooden toll bridge. The road to there was tarmac and narrow, with hawthorn hedges. After admiring the lovely view of Lancing College chapel, we would walk onto the aerodrome.

The kissing gate path was on the south side of Upper Shoreham Road, opposite our drive. This path ran south [past the Oxen field & Shoreham Court] to Mill Lane, where there were two tall sloping posts, side by side, known as the kissing gate [see photo 103]. The path had hedges. At the lower end there was high flint wall on the east side belonging to Vicarage Lodge. We played tennis there, but I hated the game. [The lower end of this path still exists as a twitten, and the position of the kissing gate is marked by a curved recess in the high flint wall.]

Mr. Fred Langrish (b.1916) lived in the surviving west part (former servants quarters) of the earlier Buckingham House, home of the Bridgers until c.1890.

I was born in Lewes in 1916 and came to Shoreham in 1925 with my mother, step-father [Mr. D. R. Paris], younger brother Malcolm, and my half brother Dick Paris. We attended Old Shoreham school. For the first few months we lived at No. 21 Old Shoreham, which is the left hand one of the three cottages which are now the Amsterdam p.h. [photo 10]. The western part of Upper Shoreham Road did not exist then. West-bound traffic went along St. Nicolas Lane, past the school, to get to the Old Shoreham toll bridge.

Lived at Buckingham House. My step-father got a job as a gardener at Buckingham park, which was a private park in those days, owned by the Harrisons. I believe Mr. Harrison owned a tannery business in Chichester. They had two sons. I believe the younger son was Peter, who was away at college. The Harrisons lived at the later Buckingham House [see photo 99], since demolished, which stood [200 yards] to the north of the earlier Buckingham House [see photo 89].

The walls [classical facades] of the earlier Buckingham House were standing at that time, but there was no roof and it was grassed over between the walls. The building then stood within the park. The walls still survive, but the public park is smaller than the old private park. The east and south walls [classical facades] are in Woodview, off Norman Crescent. We lived in the old buildings [former servants quarters] which were attached to the west side of those surviving walls.

In our time, the old buildings were divided into three dwellings. The head gardener, Barnes, and his family lived in the N.E. part, we lived in the N.W. part and the chauffeur, George Hubbard, lived in the south part. The garage was opposite him, to the south, and he washed the cars on an adjacent area of granite sets with a canopy over. The old part where we lived was demolished and is now flats.

There was a continuous brick wall along the east, north, and part of the west side of Buckingham park when we lived there, with no gates except the access from Upper Shoreham Road by the Lodge. [The brick wall was built c.1914 to keep soldiers out, but it seems they used the park later in the war.]

The Knights lived at [the later] Buckingham Lodge [see photo 91]. Mr. Russell lived at the Lodge when we first went there. The Lodge stood on the east side of the entrance to the park and Harrison's house, but the entrance to the present public park is further east. [The Lodge is now No. 324 Upper Shoreham Road.]

[From the Lodge, the drive went north, then turned east in front of the lawn, then north again to the front of the earlier house, which faced east across the park. A turn-off after the first bend led to the stables and the west side of the house, i.e. the servants quarters. The stables are now converted to dwellings.]

117

Old steam engines. When we were at school there were no houses on The Drive, just trees. About half way up the hill there were several steam traction engines which had been left there and abandoned. We used to play on them. [The Drive was formerly a drove road for moving livestock.]

Fetes in the park. There were occasions when the Harrisons let the park out for fetes and other events. Such events were usually declared open from the steps of the surviving east entrance [see photo 98].

Harrison sold out. After we had lived there for about three years, Mr. Harrison sold the property and my father-in-law lost his job. We moved to 25 Ship Street, and I was living there during my last two years at school [c.1928-1930]. Mr. Harrison's house became a school.

A brief history by R. Hill

The earlier Buckingham House was built for the Bridger family c.1820 in classical style to a design by J. B. Rebecca. It faced east across a park of about 55 acres. Around 1890, the Bridgers moved to Adur Lodge and let the house to Henry Head. A few years after he died in 1905, it was bought by W. G. Little, who built a new house 200 yards to the north between 1912 & c.1921, when E. R. Harrison purchased the property. He sold 38 acres of Buckingham park to Shoreham Council in 1930 and it was officially opened to the public in Feb. 1931.

The later Buckingham House became the Downs School, run by the Misses Wood & Cleare c. 1935. The house was sold to Brighton Corporation in 1945, when it was described as standing in 5 to 6 acres of wooded grounds. It had a large lounge, drawing room, library, billiards room, 12 bedrooms, 3 bathrooms, servants quarters, and a detached brick built hall with a stage and seating for 300. It became Buckingham House Children's Home, Ravensbourne Avenue, and was demolished in the 1960's.

The Head family. Henry Head was an underwriter from London. The family spent the summers at Buckingham House and took a lot of interest in the local community. An annual show and garden party and other events were held in the park largely at the expense of the Heads. Memorials in St. Nicolas church record the passing of Henry Head and his wife, and the tragic loss of sons: Henry Head died at Buckingham House on 1 July 1905, age 70. Hester, his wife, died at Cadogen Place in London on 6 December 1907, age 72. Francis, their fourth son, died at Buckingham House on 11 February 1905, age 37. Christopher, their 5th son, born on Christmas day 1869, was lost on the wreck of the Titanic on 15 April 1912, age 42. Bernard, their eighth son was killed in action at Gallipoli on 13 August 1915, age 39.

W. G. Little occupied Buckingham House with his wife and their two grand children, Betty and Pansy. They had a number of servants including two nurses, a nursery maid, butler, cook, tweeny maid, house boy, laundry maid, coachman, bailiff, and several gardeners. [From Adur Herald, 18 June 1982.]

Mrs. Doreen Weston (nee Virgo b.1916) lived at Pond Cottage. Her father was once a page boy at Buckingham House, and her mother was a servant at Little Buckingham house. Her grandfather Boxall was the village blacksmith.

Page boy at Buckingham House. My father, William Harvey Virgo, worked at Buckingham House as a page boy before he married. We have a photo of him in his uniform [see photo 92L]. When the Head family went to London to their town house he went with them. They spent their summers down here. When father came out of the army after the first world war he was the porter at Shoreham Grammar School. He worked there for a number of years and we lived in Pond Cottage, which was on the east side of the school. My brother, Robert Harvey Virgo, was born there in 1920. By the time I started at Old Shoreham school, in September 1921, we were living at 2 Commercial Terrace, Old Shoreham Road, which is near the Swiss Cottage p.h. It is a three storey house, now known as 22 Old Shoreham Road.

Lots of Virgos. I think my father came from Portslade, but my mother, Elisabeth, was from Shoreham. Her maiden name was also Virgo. She was a domestic servant at Little Buckingham farmhouse before she married. My grandmother always said that old Sam Virgo, who lived in Fishersgate, had seven sons, that they all had families, and so the Virgo family spread out.

Brought up by grandmother Boxall. Mother died when I was age 5 and Robert was 18 months. My grandmother, Sarah Ann Boxall, brought us up at 2 Commercial Terrace; adjacent to the Young's sweet shop at the corner of Buckingham Street. Their daughter was a teacher at Old Shoreham school.

Boxall the blacksmith. My grandfather, John Boxall, was the village blacksmith and operated from the old tin shed which stood on the west side of Old Shoreham Road, opposite Upper Shoreham Road [see photo 68]. I believe grandfather died before I was born. [The building is marked marked 'Sm.' on the 1912 map. The 1901 directory lists J. Boxall, shoeing & general smith.]

Farmer Redman complained. If the weather was bad, the quickest way to school was up Old Shoreham Road and across Charlie Miller's field. If the weather was good we liked to go via Freehold Street and the cinder path, which is now Connaught Avenue. There were orchards on the left [S.W.] side of the cinder path, and corn or root crops on the other side, such as mangel-wurzel. We sometimes scrumped in the orchards, played in the corn, or pulled up a mangel-wurzel. The farmer, Mr. Redman, sometimes complained to the school.

Domestic service then Land Army. I left school at 14 [1930] and went into domestic service for the Christie's at Windlesham Gardens. I was nanny to the children and I did all kinds of domestic work. I was in the Land Army during the war, first at Ifield for a few years, then with Teddy Burfoot, who had the nursery [market garden] along Middle Road. Hammy Lane was just a cart track then. I worked there until I married in 1946, then continued part time.

119

My dear Father,

I came down here yesterday morning to pick up my strength and, as the only member of the family present at the great catastrophe of this morning, I am attempting to give you some idea of the misfortune that has come to the Squire and indirectly upon us:

It blew hard last night but seemed to abate somewhat about early morning. Only some rotten branches were blown from the trees. At about 10 a.m., in beautiful weather, it somewhat rapidly increased, blowing hard from the S.W. Apart from the wind, it was so pleasant that I was out in ordinary clothes, without a hat, smoking a pipe. Then the sound of the wind grew to a roar like many steam locomotives going by. With a noise exactly like the firing of a great gun, one of the big trees came down across the drive [see photo 97]. I was standing in the field and saw it fall. It was rapidly followed by another and then they came down in two's and three's, smashing the fencing and the shrubbery as they fell.

Within half an hour 20 big trees had fallen and there were four great barriers across the drive. The trees were not broken but torn up by the roots, leaving huge holes in the land four to six feet deep. We then heard the noise, like cannon, from the back and [we] all went into the garden. Alfred announced that a tree had fallen across the kennel, so we all went into the garden to try and save the dogs [hounds]. We had the gate into the orchard open when I looked up and saw a kind of rocking movement in the whole of the row of elms on the west side of the park. I shouted 'Run - the trees are falling' but we were all knocked down by the tops of the elms as they broke over the wall which separates the garden from the orchard, fowl house & kennels. Alfred, Pratt, Hart [head gardener] and I all received bruises or cuts but no-one was a bit the worse.

Seventeen trees had come down exactly like ninepins, destroying the fowl house and kennels and reducing the orchard to the condition of a timber merchant's lumber yard. As we picked ourselves up and got clean we looked in the direction of the library gable of the house. Suddenly all the ilex trees which hide that corner of the house from the garden disappeared. They did not go with a great crash like the elms but simply sank away, leaving blue sky & clean cut gable visible. It was all like a curious transformation scene. It just began to sway & the gale blew harder than ever so we went out to view the west side of the park from the apple lawn. Nineteen trees then fell in the space between the hunting gate and the kennels. Thus 36 trees were uprooted, besides many branches that were destroyed, on the west side of the park only. All the five elms in sight of mother's bedroom window went early in the storm. I was standing by the rail at the time and saw them give a curious kind of lift then topple over exactly like a set of ninepins; when you think you have missed the corner pin but yet he is really grazed and all the others fall in answer. The following is a list of the fallen trees.

Drive and immediate neighbourhood	20	
West side of park (end of the stable to end of kennels)	17	
West side of park (end of kennels to hunting gate)	19	
In the park - scattered	3	
- directly opposite front door	5	
Big ilex trees etc. in garden (west of croquet lawn)	8	
In the Triangle [north end of Buckingham Road]	10	Total 82

The results are most astounding. In two hours the place was transformed. You can now see the red brick back to the house from the croquet lawn. Looking to the west from the walled garden there are no trees and many other queer changes have occurred.

All the dogs were found safe but several hens, who were laying, were guillotined. They apparently poked their heads out of their nests and the falling roof [slates] cut their heads off. Many slates are gone and the lead edging is lifted as if a giant hand had scratched it up and twisted it. The house is otherwise intact but the library window is completely blocked with fallen trees. Some glass has been broken in the hot houses but fortunately no tree fell onto them. Hart kept on saying in his somewhat stupid way 'It tisn't the elms - they're no good - it's them ilex oaks I'm sorry for' - until I was sick of this remark. It was not until after lunch that it dawned upon his stupid mind that his orchard with all his prize fruit trees was absolutely wiped out of existence. He is now nearly crying with anger and 'them ilex oaks' have quite disappeared from his conversation, to my great relief.

Luckin's barns and ricks [Old Shoreham farm] are destroyed - and the end of the new soap works has been blown in, but otherwise not much other land damage has been done. The chemical works, like a secretive old maid, say they have suffered but are secret as to the extent, nature and situation.

I have entirely cut you out [up-staged you]. The park this afternoon has been crowded with the Villa folk old & young. I conduct all the older ones round the show in a definite order - telling the same stories and making the same remarks at the same spots. I particularly fascinated the Dells, I believe, who thanked me for the 'privilege' of being allowed to see 'how extensive havoc has been wrought by the gale'.

Mrs. Bridger sends her love to mother - she also has been for the tour under my guidance. I am sending you some photographs on Saturday (March 6). I shall probably write again shortly. [Photo 97 is one of the photographs.]

With much love, Great affection. Henry Head.

Mr. David Webb (b.1941) of Lancing is the son of Nellie Webb (nee Turrell). The Turrell family have had a continuous presence in Old Shoreham since 1820 or earlier.

My mother, born in 1914, was christened Ivy Gladys Nellie Turrell but is known as 'Nellie'. She is still alive but unable to give an interview. Her father, George Turrell, was born in Old Shoreham c.1880. Her grandfather Thomas Turrell was born in Old Shoreham c.1849, and his father, also Thomas, was born at Old Erringham c.1820. [Thomas probably lived at Old Erringham cottages, see photo 84.]

Thomas Turrell [born c.1849], her grandfather, lived to age 87. His wife was Christiana Reeves [1850-1933]. Her father was Captain John Reeves, a master mariner of Southwick, whose brigantine 'Nelson' was lost off Scarborough with all hands in 1864.

Lived at Hoopers Cottages for 60 years. Thomas and Christiana lived at No. 4 Hoopers Cottages for nearly 60 years prior to her death in 1933. That was the west cottage which is now part of the Amsterdam p.h. We have a photo of them sitting inside the cottage in 1931 [see photo 109]. Christiana's brother, Harry Reeves of Victoria Road, was the toll collector on the Norfolk Bridge.

Thomas was the second of seven children, all boys, and all born at Erringham or Old Shoreham. Their names and approximate dates of birth (from census returns) were Wolter (1845), Thomas (1849), Charles (1851), William (1853), George (1855), Frederick (1858) and Samuel (1861).

Brother fell from chapel roof. Samuel, a labourer, helped to build Lancing College chapel and was killed in 1884, at age 23, when he fell off the roof. He is buried at St. Nicolas church, Old Shoreham. His grave stone is on the right, just north of the lych gate.

Thomas scared the rooks away. Thomas was interviewed by the Lancing & Shoreham Times soon after his wife died. He was born at Erringham farm, had no 'schooling', and started work at the age of nine or ten, keeping rooks off the corn at Old Shoreham and Little Buckingham farms. After that, he worked for Squire Gorringe of Kingston for a few years. According to the press report, he walked from Erringham farm to Kingston every morning and had to work until very late. The highest paid workers [carters] at that time got only 13 shillings [65p] a week, and had to start at 4 a.m. to get the horses ready. Thomas next worked at Erringham farm for Mr. Sharpe [Richard Sharpe was the farmer at Erringham 1847-66].

Became a ships carpenter. Thomas was twice apprenticed to ship-building, helping to build vessels at Shoreham and learning carpentry with Mr. May and Mr. Dyer. My uncle Harry says that Thomas worked at Stow's yard, and still had his tools after he retired. He says the tools were in two boxes, and the top of one was shaped so that he could sit on it while he was doing certain kinds of work. He often used an adze. [From the press report] Thomas worked on the railways as a carpenter for 26 years, but that was not his last job. He travelled around for the railway, but he lived in Old Shoreham for all except the last few years of his life.

Helped re-build the toll bridge. Some time after he had left the railway, he went back to help re-build Old Shoreham toll bridge. He helped put in the new piles. [The London Brighton & South Coast Railway Company completely rebuilt the bridge during the 1914-18 war, but followed the design of the original bridge which opened in 1782.]

Thomas had eight children. The first three were born at New Shoreham and the others at Old Shoreham. Their names and approximate dates of birth were Ellen (1872), Mary (1874), Thomas (1877), George (1880), Hugh (1882), Annie (1885), Rosetta (1889), and Charles c.1892. Charles was killed in the first world war and his name is on the memorial list in St. Nicolas church, Old Shoreham. [See war memorial lists on page 125].

George Turrell, born 1880, and Emily Catherine (nee Shiner) were my mother's parents. The family lived at No. 7 Aston Cottages, off Freehold Street, until it was demolished in the 1950's. [G. Turrell is listed there in the 1914 & 1954 directories]. George, my grandfather, worked at the Beeding cement works for probably 30 years. The Shiners lived on Freehold Street, then moved to Old Shoreham Road. [Listed at 3 Freehold Street in 1914; 79 Old Shoreham Road 1930 & 1954.]

Nellie Turrell, my mother, had four older brothers; George (b.1904), Charles (b.1906), Harry (b.1908), and Frank (b.1911). Harry is her only surviving brother. Frank lived on Adur Avenue from 1938 and worked in the building trade. His wife, Elizabeth, who still lives on Adur Avenue, did part-time domestic work at Greystones for Mr. & Mrs. James for many years.

Nellie's mother died. Mother attended Old Shoreham school until she was 14 years old [1928] and received excellent reports. She attended Sunday School at St. Nicolas church and sang in the choir in her teens and early 20's. Her mother died at age 55 in 1928, within a week of my mother's 14th birthday. After leaving school, mother kept house for her father and her older brother George. Consequently, because of her selflessness, she never went out to work or pursued a career.

My mother met my father, Lewis, in 1937 at one of the dances held regularly then at St. Mary's hall. They were married in 1938 at Old Shoreham church. My sister Iris and I were christened there in 1940 and 1942 respectively.

Even after my mother was married she continued to do a lot for my grandfather and uncle, and I remember going with her and my sister to Shoreham on countless occasions in the forties and fifties. Shoreham was different then - life was lived at a slower pace and people seemed more contented.

Memories in order of appearance

The images reproduced in this volume came from the following collections:

Lost in action in the 1914-18 war

Herbert G. Bishop

Henry V. Christmas

Thomas F. R. English

A. R. Haig-Brown

William E. Kimmens

Harold Standen

Alfred H. Standing

Charles S. Turrell

William A. Weller

Lost in action in the 1939-45 war

Rodney Akehurst

Arthur Ayland

Ralph Barnes

Walter Bowyer

Albert Brown

Walter Cook

Mervyn Curd

Albert Cuthbert

John Dawson

George Earthey

George Farmer

T. L. Fasson

Digby Gates

Peter Gates

Ronald Glazebrook

Kenneth Gilbert

William Gunn

James Hackett

John Hayman

John Hoad

Sidney Hoad

Ernest Husband

C. Knight

John Laker

Albert Lisher

William Mackie

Albert Maynard

Ainslee Merses

Charles Nye

John Page

Wilfred Parsons

Reginald Payne

Ernest Portlock

Gerald Prince

Raymond Roberts

Benjamin Saunders

Deborah Shute

Raymond Smith

Maurice Steele

James Steer

Ronald Stillwell

Arthur Stoner

Gordon Terry

Raymond Tuppen

Sydney Walter

Roy Welch

Robert Wells

C. George Wheeler

Stanley Wheeler

George West

Joseph Woods

Joseph Young.

The above lists are taken from the memorials in St. Nicolas church, Old Shoreham, Shoreham-by-Sea, West Sussex.

Name index for both volumes

Adams 1 photo 73
Akehurst 125
Alexander 85
Archer 13 15 37
  43 50 78
  photo 18
Avis 106
Ayland 125
Ayling 20 40 94
Bailey 109
Baker 70 79
  photos 33 72
Barker photo 72
Barnardo 14
Barnes 117 125
Bartlett 25 26 27
  46 97 99 101
  photo 3
Barton 95
Bates 28 91
  photo 19
Batten 12 24 47 56
  62 63 106
Bazen 70 108
Benson 86
Berridge 40
Biggs 113
Bishop 20 33 40
  53 57 65 70 94 116 125
  photos 40 71
Blackwood 43
Bobby 106
Boreham 42
Bowers 64
Bowthorpe 94
Bowyer 37 78 85
  124 125
  photos 71 72 73
Boxall 7 17 41 84 119
  photo 68
Braose 2
Bradford 97 99 103
Bridger 2 8 19 20 23
  36 43 52 86 104 107
  117 118 120 121
photos 44 89

Bridle 81
Broadbridge 18 44
Brown 25 125
Bulloch 91
Burfoot 43 47 119
Burstow 107
Burtenshaw 43
Castle 36 72 77 80
  photo 73
Challon 62
Chandler 97 99 103
Chaplin 11 39 68
  photo 35
Cheal 53 65
Cheesman 67 68
Chewter 91
Child 79
Christie 119
Christmas 12 125
Clark 105
Cleare 118
Clements 24
Cobby photo 69
Cook 125
Colquhoun 124
Cooper 78 79
  photo 71 72
Cotman 27 87 90 92
Cox photo 72
Curd 21 125
Cuthbert 125
Dawson 125
Daynes 98
Dell 82 121
Denton photos 71 72
Divers 40 98
Dobson 99
Dorey 47
  photos 72 73
Dove 16
Duke 70 94 photo 3
Dye photo 72
Dyer 122
Eade 97
Eames 29 70
  photo 33

Eager 105
  photo 83
Earthey 125
Elliott 70 124
Ellman-Brown 12 36 104
  photo 44
Elms 11
Emney 104
English 125
Evans 64
Everest photo 72
Farmer 125
Farr 110
Fasson 125
Fenix 102
Firth-kettle 28 46 84
Flinn 38
Frampton 4 5 7 14 15
  16 29 38 39 40 41 42
  45 47 48 73 74 75 76
  98 100 106 112
  photos 24 29 30 31 32
Froggatt 42
Frost 75
Frith 15 photo 20
Fry 60
Fuller 4 17 21 39 45
  49 53 57 59 62 64
  65 68 83 109 110 111
  112 116
  photos 13 14 45 50
  55 57 59 71 72 73
Funnell 24 77
Gadd 81 82 photo 73
Gamman 94
Gates 101 125
Gawn photo 72
Gilbert 27 43 92 125
Giles 95
Glazebrook 71 125
Glew photos 71 72
Glover 60
Glossop 37 45 50 78
Glyde 78
Godley 43 photo 73
Godsmark 92

Name index for both volumes

Goldsmith 40
Gorringe 122
Grinstead photos 71 73
Grossmark 4 5 68
Gumbrill 45 70
Gunn 125
Gunning 107
Hackett 125
Haig-Brown 125
Hamilton photo 73
Hancorn 79 photo 71
Harmsworth 24
Harrison 114 117 118
  photo 99
Hart 120 121
Hatcher 87
Hayman 125
Head 118 119 120 121
  photos 89 92R 93
Heather photo 72
Hecks 5 11
Hemsley 48
Henbrey 51
Hersey photo 72
Hoad 125
Hoare 70 124
Holloway 75
Holmes 70 110
  photo 60
Hooker 24
House 36 98
Hubbard 117
Hughes 78
Hunt 19 107 photo 73
Husband 125
Hyne 36
Jackson 78
James 11 39 40 42
  115 123
  photo 37
Jenner 92 124
Johnson photos 71 73
Johnstone photo 73
Jones 15 photo 20
Jordan photos 71 72

Kay 96
Kemp 21
Kelly 57 61 110 115
Kennedy 40
Kent 68 photo 40
Kimmens 125
Kinloch 39
Knight 62 64 75
  117 125
  photos 71 73
Laker 125
Lanning 21
Langrish 79 117
  photos 71 72
Lawrence 14 15 40
  photo 38
Lea 114 115
Lee 12 29
Leggett 4 68 124
Leney 25
Lillywhite 13 87
Lisher 125
Little 42 118 photo 99
Longley 6 47 75
  photo 26
Luckin 121
Lucking 19
Luther 57 110
  photo 57
McIlroy 91
Mackie 125
MacLeod 79
MacNab 40
Margo 40
Mason 12 16 28 39
  41 73 103
  photos 19 25 36L
Matthews 20 23 104
  photo 73
May 122
Mayler 110
Maynard 125
Mayne 104
Merses 125
Miles 91

Milham 81
Millard 36
Miller 17 20 34 37
  43 72 86 119
Minter 79
  photos 72 73
Moore 68
Munnery 21 32 33 36
  photos 11 12 42 72 73
Newman 112
Norfolk, Duke of, 2 83
Norman photos 69 70
Northeast 84
Nye 8 53 58 59 60 62
  65 66 90 111 125
Oakman photo 75
Osborne 57 photos 55 57
Packham 21 38 68 124
Page 49 125
Paris 117 photo 73
Parker 104
Parlett 41 107
Parsons 26 125
Pascoe 96
Passmore 7 45 76 97
  99 100 124
Patching 14 19 24
Payne 15 16 27 103 125
Peacock 49
Perham 17 43
  photos 71 72 73
Perkins 72 79
Perryman 3 17 23 27
  34 43 46 72 87 88
  89 92 93 124
  photos 10 66 74R 75
Peters photo 71
Pierce 68 124
Piper 19
Plumb 99 photo 104
Pool 111
Porter photo 44
Portlock 125
Porton 19
Povey 68 124

127

Name index for both volumes

Pratt 120
Pretty 77 photo 72
Priest 103 photo 71
Prince 77 79 125
  photo 72
Puckett 85
Puttock 19 photo 73
Pycroft 71 124
Rawlings 16 40 95 99
  100 101 103 124
  photos 76-78
Rebecca 118
Redman 5 7 41 119
Reeves 122
Ricardo 5
Richardson 79
Roberts 125
Robertson-Aikman 46
Robins 79
Rook photo 44
Rothwell 40 83
Row 62 64
Russell 117
Samuelson 11
Sanders photo 73
Sanford 82
Sargent 83
Saunders 125
  photos 71 72 73
Sayers 57 62 63 116
  photos 55 57 58
Scott 110
Selby 32 33 36
Sharpe 112 122
Shelley 42 98
Shiner 123
Short 49 110
Shute 125
Simpson 42
Sinden 109
  photos 71 73
Slater 24 34 71
  photo 16
Slaughter 103

Smart 85 94
Smith 36 77 80 125
  photo 73
Snelling 70 68 87
Snook 85 86
  photos 71 72
Spackman 7 24 44 48
Spiers 53 110 116
Spragg 15 43 51 78
  photo 18
Stamp image 80
Standen 125
Standing 20 125
Steele 125
Steer 125
Stenning 20 81 82
Stephens photo 44
Stevens 7 10
Still photos 71 73
Stillwell 125
Stone 24
Stoner 28 46 99 102 125
Stow 13 122
Strivens 83 100
Suter photo 71
Tamplin 20 55
Tapner 19
Tates 94
Terry 125
Tester 97 99 101 103
Thomas 1 11 23
  photo 31R
Tingley photos 69 70
Topham 43
Tompsett photos 71 72
Torr 4 6 18 41 45 47
  51 53 54 57 58 59 60
  61 64 65 68 107 109
  111 112 113 115
  photos 46 54R 61 62
  63 64
Towner 19 photo 2
Trigwell 111
Tubb 81

Tuppen 6 16 21 27 31
  32 34 41 43 45 47 52
  54 56 70 75 107
  109 111 116 125
  photos 5 6 71 72
Turner photo 57
Turrell 122 125
  photo 109
Upton 44 68 124
Uridge 24
Virgo 119
  photos 92L 71 72
Wadey 96 photo 77
Walker 100
Walter 125
Watts 97
Webb 122 124
Welch 125
Weller 16 17 19 25 29
  34 39 68 125
  photos 33 43
Wells 19 125
  photos 43 73
Wellstead 82 photo 71
West 125
Weston 119 124
Wetherhead 16 17 26
Wheeler 125
White 37 photos 72 73
Wickham photo 73
Wiffin 57 58 61 64
  110 111 115
Windle 95
Winter photo 10
Winton 42 44
  photo 41
Witten 70 124
Wood 118
Woods 125
Woolmington 7 41 43
  photos 72 73
Upton 44
Young 13 15 43
  68 78 119
  125 photo 18

General index to both volumes

General index to both volumes

General index to both volumes

General index to both volumes